SHORT COURSE SERIES

Clockwise
pre-intermediate

Classbook

D1295553

Bruce McGowen &
Vic Richardson

OXFORD
UNIVERSITY PRESS

Contents

01 BEING ME

Speak for yourself

1 Complete these sentences in as many different ways as possible.

I come from Barcelona / Spain / a big family.

1. I come from ...
2. I was born in ...
3. My family ...
4. I work / study ...
5. I live ...
6. I've never ...
7. One day I'd like to ...

2 In pairs. Compare your ideas and ask questions.

Grammar

Question forms

1 Read the texts about Sarah and George. Match these headings to the paragraphs. Which heading is used twice?

- My future
- My daughter
- My family
- My home
- My work
- My free time

2 How are they similar or different to you?

Sarah Brown, 28, lives in Eastbourne with her daughter Kate.

1 _____

Kate's five. When my husband and I split up three years ago we decided she should have two homes. So now she stays with him in his flat from Sunday to Tuesday, and with me from Wednesday to Saturday. She's a happy little girl – she loves going to school and telling me how to run my life!

2 _____

I live in a small two-bedroom house which I bought two years ago. It's in a quiet neighbourhood very near the town centre. I'm spending every evening and weekend decorating it at the moment.

3 _____

When I finished university I wanted to be an artist, but then I had Kate. I always wanted to be a long-distance lorry driver when I was young, but now I'm an assistant manager in a hotel. It's not a very interesting job but it pays well and the holidays are good.

4 _____

I don't really have any plans for the future. I've done what I wanted to do, like travelling, being a wild student, and becoming a mum. What more could I ask for?

George Conway, 24, lives in Winnipeg, Canada, with his parents and his brother Bruce.

5 _____

I finished college last year, and I started a temporary job at Winnipeg Public Library. I've been offered a permanent job, but I'm going to go back to university.

6 _____

I spend a lot of time on the net, talking to people, designing web pages, or just surfing around. Maybe I'm a bit of a nerd! I have a girlfriend, Robyn – it's not serious yet, but we go out together two or three times a week. You'd be surprised what you can do in Winnipeg, even when it's 40 degrees below. Because it's so isolated we have our own symphony orchestra and our own opera company, and we have more restaurants per capita than any city in North America.

7 _____

My dad's getting old now but he's still quite active. He worked for Manitoba Heat and Light until he retired, and now he annoys my mom because he's around the house all day. My mom was a teacher and she still sometimes does some substitute teaching. My brother Bruce is a bit of a nerd too, but he gets paid for it – he's a computer engineer.

3 Cover the texts and complete these sentences. Which ones have an auxiliary verb?

1 Kate _____ with her father for three days a week.

2 Sarah _____ every evening decorating her house.

3 She and her husband _____ three years ago.

4 Sarah _____ what she wanted to do.

5 George _____ work at the library last year.

6 He _____ to go back to university.

7 You _____ do a lot in Winnipeg.

8 George's dad _____ old.

4 Make the sentences into Yes/No questions. Which need a new word?

Does Kate stay with her father for three days a week?

Question forms

1 Complete these rules by choosing the correct words. Choose examples from the questions in exercise 4.

1 If a sentence has an auxiliary verb, we make a question by putting the auxiliary verb *before/ after* the subject.

e.g. _____

2 If a sentence doesn't have an auxiliary verb, we make a question with *be/ do*.

e.g. _____

Remember that if a question has *do*, *does*, or *did*, the main verb is the infinitive.

e.g. _____

2 In pairs. Correct the mistakes in these sentences.

1 A Do Sarah live in Eastbourne?
  B Yes, she lives.

2 When you are going to finish university?

3 A Do you have been to Paris?
  B Yes, I do.

4 A Your brothers and sisters are married?
  B Yes, they married.

5 When did you started studying English?

6 How often does George and Robyn go out?

Practice

1 Match these question words with the answers.

What	In Winnipeg.
Where	Two years ago.
Who	Because it's so isolated.
When	She's an assistant manager.
Why	Two or three times a week.
How much	His parents and his brother.
How often	£22,000 a year.

2 In pairs. What are the complete questions about Sarah and George? Ask and answer.

3 Put these words in the correct order to make questions.
1 last what do did night you
2 English you studying are why
3 last where you for go holiday did your
4 free like doing do in you your what time
5 this what going do weekend to you are
6 like to you the UK would live in

4 In pairs. Ask and answer questions 1–6. Ask follow-up questions.

5 Against the clock `5 minutes` Ask your partner questions to get these answers. Tick (✓) each answer when you hear it.

Have you got a mobile phone?

Yes, I have. ✓	No, I haven't.	Yes, I was.	No, I wasn't.
Yes, I do.	No, I don't.	Yes, I did.	No, I didn't.
Yes, I am.	No, I'm not.	Yes, I can.	No, I can't.
I don't know.	That's rather a personal question!		

If someone asks you a question which you don't want to answer, e.g. 'Are you rich?', say 'That's rather a personal question!'

Can you remember ...?
• how to make questions and short answers
• six things about George Conway
• five words or phrases you can use to talk about yourself
Practice p.84

Speak out

1 Your teacher will write five answers to *Wh-* questions about herself / himself. Try to ask questions for the answers.

2 Write down five answers of your own. Work in pairs and try to ask the right questions.

02
SOCIAL LIFE

Speak for yourself

1 What do you like doing in your spare time? What sort of person are you? (The answer could be 'both' or 'neither'.)
- a cinema person or a video person?
- a restaurant person or an eat-at-home person?
- a television person or a book person?
- an indoor person or an outdoor person?
- a sport person or a culture person?
- a solitary person or a sociable person?

2 **In groups.** Compare your ideas. Are you similar?

Vocabulary
Staying in and going out

 1 **Against the clock** 3 minutes Add these activities to the word web. Can you think of any more?

watch TV	go for a walk	go to a football match
go out for dinner	surf the net	go to the pub
chat on the phone	play tennis	have dinner with friends
go to a sports centre	get a take-away	read a book
go to the cinema	go to a nightclub	have an early night

an evening in
watch TV

STAYING IN AND GOING OUT

an active weekend

a first date
go out for dinner

2 Which things do you do most often?

English in use
Social arrangements

1 Look at this dialogue and complete the missing lines. Where are Oliver and Holly going?

are you going	this evening	to come	and pick you up
near the station	7.30	be nice	nothing special

Oliver	Are you doing anything _____ ?
Holly	No, _____ .
Oliver	Well, we're going to that new Chinese restaurant _____ . Would you like _____ ?
Holly	Yes, that would _____ . What time _____ ?
Oliver	About 8.00. Shall we come _____ ?
Holly	Yes, great.
Oliver	OK, I'll call for you at _____ .

We use the present continuous to talk about arrangements. We always use a time reference, e.g. *this evening, this weekend, next week, next month, tomorrow*. Find an example in the dialogue.

2 ⊙1 Listen and check your ideas.

3 ⊙2 Listen to two more dialogues. What decisions do the people make?

4 ⊙3 You don't always want to accept an invitation. Listen to these four dialogues.
   1 What phrases do the people use for refusing the invitations?
   2 What reasons do they give?

Useful language

1 Listen to the dialogues in exercises 3 and 4 again and tick (✓) the expressions you hear.

Invitations and suggestions	Accepting	Refusing
Would you like + infinitive?	That would be nice.	I'm (really) sorry, but I can't. I'm + -ing ...
Do you fancy + -ing?	That would be great.	I'm afraid I can't. I have to ...
How about + -ing?	Good idea!	I'd love to, but I ...
Shall we + verb?	Great idea!	I don't really like ...
Let's + verb	I'd love to.	I'm afraid I'm a bit busy.
Why don't we + verb?	Fine.	How about ... instead?
	Yes, OK.	
	That's a good idea.	

2 🕐 **Against the clock** [3 minutes] How many invitations and suggestions can you make?

Shall we go for a walk?   Would you like to go for a walk?   Do you fancy going for a walk?

go	to go	going	a coffee	a sandwich
play	to play	playing	for a walk	tennis
have	to have	having	a take-away	to the cinema

Practice

1 How are these words pronounced?

shall we
are you
do you
would you

 2 Now listen to them in sentences. How are they pronounced? Repeat them and try to sound exactly the same.

Shall we go to the theatre?
Are you doing anything this evening?
Do you fancy a take-away?
Would you like to see the new musical?

Always try to give a reason when refusing an invitation.

Can you remember ...?

• two different ways of making invitations and suggestions
• two expressions for refusing invitations
• ten free time activities

Practice p.85

3 **In pairs.** Make short dialogues with invitations and suggestions. Accept some and refuse others.

A *Do you fancy going out for dinner?*
B *Yes, that would be nice.*
A *Where shall we go?*

• go out for dinner
• stay in this evening
• go out
• go to the pub
• go to see a film
• go to a football match
• go to Edinburgh for the weekend

Speak out

1 Think about things you would like to do this weekend. Decide what, where, and when.

2 **In pairs.** Make dates and social arrangements by following the arrows in the chart.

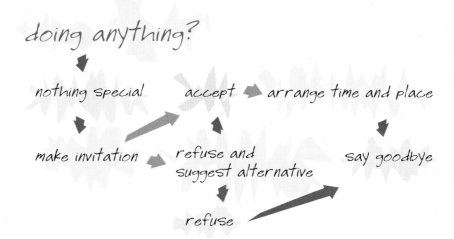

doing anything?

nothing special   accept ➡ arrange time and place

make invitation ➡ refuse and suggest alternative   say goodbye

refuse

3 Practise your dialogues and perform them for the class.

03
MEET THE FAMILY

In this lesson

- Family vocabulary
- Describing people
- Compound adjectives

Speak for yourself

1 Complete the family members of the five generations.

2 **In pairs.** How many of these things are you?

older	grandfather	grandm _____	(= gr _____)		
↕	fa _____	mo _____	(= p _____)	un _____	au _____
	br _____	si _____	**YOU**	co _____	
	so _____	da _____	(= ch _____)	ne _____	ni _____
younger	gr _____	gr _____	(= gr _____)		

Vocabulary

Describing people

1 Read the texts. What family members do you think the people are describing? Match the pictures to the texts.

> He's everything I'm not! He's very tall and slim, he's got dark hair, and he's confident, outgoing, and good at sports. Luckily, he's no good at school – I'm the intelligent one ...

> She's still very young, and she's a gorgeous little kid. She's got curly ginger hair, and she's really lively and friendly. People say she's got her mother's eyes, but I think she looks more like me ...

> He's quite old now, in his seventies I think, but he's never gone bald. He's got short grey hair (he calls it 'silver') and glasses. He's fairly quiet. He's always been quite thin, and he was probably very good-looking when he was young.

2 Underline the words connected with appearance and personality.

1 Add them to the chart.

hair	height + build	age	looks	personality
	tall			

2 **Against the clock** 3 minutes Add these words to the chart.

skinny   a teenager   attractive   middle-aged   a beard   a moustache
shy   blonde   fair   in his/her twenties   elderly   straight

Be careful with words like *thin* and *skinny* – they can sound negative. *Slim* is better.

3 Can you find any opposites in the chart? Can you add any more words?

Look at the texts again. What four words make the adjectives stronger or weaker?

stronger _____ _____

weaker _____ _____

4 Listen. Repeat the words and sentences.

5 **In pairs.** A gives B a word from the chart, and B makes a sentence with *He's / She's (a) ...* or *He's got / She's got (a) ...* Then change over.

   A *beard*

   B *He's got a beard.*

6 Which descriptions do these sentences go with? Check the meaning of the parts in italics.

   1 *I get on with him really well* – he likes telling me about when he was young.

   2 *I don't look like him at all* – people can't believe we're brothers.

   3 *She takes after her mother* in lots of ways – she never does anything she doesn't want to.

Practice

1 Imagine you are arranging to meet a relative you have never met. Describe yourself so that they can recognize you.

If you don't know how old someone is, you can say e.g. *25-ish* or *40-ish*.

Can you remember ...?
- ten family members
- five adjectives to describe personality
- ten adjectives to describe appearance

Practice p.85

Compound adjectives	*Extra!*

a You can make *hair* and *eye* into adjectives, e.g. *dark-haired*, *blue-eyed*. Can you make more adjectives like this?

left-	fair-	green-	hot-	narrow-	broad-	short-
blooded	shouldered	haired	sighted	handed	eyed	minded

b Check the meaning. Which adjectives describe personality? Which ones describe you or someone you know?

2 Describe someone in your class or a famous person. The class must guess the person you are describing.

Speak out

1 **In pairs.** Draw your family tree, and tell your partner something about the people in it.

2 Now make sentences with *look like*, *take after*, and *get on with*.

I look like my _____ . Both of us / Neither of us ...

I don't look like my _____ because ...

I take after my _____ because ...

I don't take after my _____ because ...

I get on with my _____ because ...

I don't get on with my _____ because ...

04 NEAREST & DEAREST

In this lesson

- Relationships vocabulary
- Listening: different relationships
- Describing relationships

Listen for yourself

Who are they?

1 🔘1 Look at this diagram. Listen to Maria describing it.

1 Who are the people?

2 Give each group a heading.

colleagues		PEOPLE I KNOW		
Jack	Norman and Maureen		John	Stella
Phil	Mrs Anderson		Louise	Mark
Colin Sanders			Sam	Julia
			Muffin	

2 Make a similar diagram for yourself. Use different headings if you like.

3 In pairs. Talk about your diagrams.

Vocabulary

Relationships

1 Look at the pictures. Which words go with each picture?

fall in love with	get on well with	get married to
get divorced from	split up with	go out with
fancy	argue with	love

2 Which of the things above could you do with these people?

1 your boyfriend / girlfriend

2 your boss

3 your brother / sister

4 your neighbour

5 your husband / wife

Listen 2

My best friend

 1 Listen to these people talking about relationships.

    1 What relationships are they talking about? Which one isn't real?

    2 Listen again. Can you find two or three key words in each description which tell you the relationship?

relationship	key words
1	
2	
3	
4	
5	

Did you notice ...?

a phrase which means
I knew her and she knew me.

Check in Tapescript 4.2.

Practice p.86

2 Which relationships do these sentences go with?

  a *A lot of our friends have split up, but I don't think we will.*

  b *We sometimes go for a drink after work.*

  c *She often wakes me up at 6.00 asking for her breakfast.*

  d *They never have noisy parties or anything.*

  e *It's not impossible, is it?*

Speak out

1 Think of three relationships of your own. They can be real or imaginary, family members, girlfriend / boyfriend, colleagues, neighbours, or anything else. Think about these things.

How long have you known them?

How often do you see them?

What are they like?

What do they look like?

Do you get on well? Why / Why not?

2 **In groups.** Describe your relationships. Ask and answer questions.

05
BEING A TRAVELLER

In this lesson

- Past simple and continuous
- Regular and irregular verbs
- Talking about travel experiences

Speak for yourself

1 Look at the map of Africa and mark these countries.
Sudan   Tanzania   Ethiopia   South Africa

2 What do you know about these places? What would travelling in Africa be like?

Grammar

Past simple and continuous

1 Look at the picture and the words in the box. What do you think the text is about?

a herd of elephants	Cape Town	temperature	a cobra
bees	litres	the Egyptian military	pasta
chocolate cake	border	illness	

2 Read the text quickly and check your ideas.

Heat, cold, mountains, deserts, illness, and animals. All of these were possible dangers when Nick Bourne decided to run from one end of Africa to the other — a journey that many people thought was impossible.

Bourne began his run in northern Egypt in October 1997. His adventure nearly ended 500 miles later while he was waiting to cross the Sudanese border — the Egyptian military stopped him and refused to let him leave the country.

Eventually, he flew to Cape Town and started again on 21 January 1998. Every day he got up at 3.30 a.m., ate a breakfast of cereal, and started running. After 20 miles he stopped for a rest and had a pasta lunch, before running another 20 miles. He drank up to 15 litres of liquid a day.

He had some incredible experiences. He was crossing the Kalahari Desert in temperatures of 62°C when he came face to face with a giant cobra. In Zambia his heartbeat went up from 135 a minute to over 190, and his doctor found that he had malaria. He saw lions and ran through a herd of elephants, and a swarm of bees attacked him while he was running through Tanzania. He celebrated his 28th birthday with a chocolate cake in the shadow of Kilimanjaro.

After eleven months and 6,021 miles he arrived at the Pyramids and finished perhaps the most amazing run ever.

20 miles = 32 kilometres

3 Read the text again. Put these events in order.

- [ ] He saw a snake.
- [ ] He decided to start from South Africa.
- [1] He started for the first time.
- [ ] He arrived at the Pyramids.
- [ ] He started for the second time.
- [ ] A swarm of bees attacked him.
- [ ] He became ill.
- [ ] He crossed the border into Egypt.
- [ ] He celebrated his birthday.
- [ ] He flew to Cape Town.

4 Against the clock `5 minutes` Find all the past simple verbs in the story. Can you divide them into regular and irregular verbs?

5 Look at this sentence. What tenses are the two verbs?

He *was crossing* the Kalahari when he *came* face to face with a giant cobra.

6 Find two more examples like this in the text.

Past simple and continuous

Form

Complete the tables with the verb *run*.

Past simple

+ I / You / He / She / It / We / They ran.

− _____ run.

? _____ run?

Past continuous

+ I / He / She / It _____ running.
You / We / They _____ running.

− I / He / She / It _____ .
You / We / They _____ .

? _____ ?
_____ ?

Use

1 Look at the example and complete the rules with *finished* and *continuing*.

He **was running** through Zambia when he **saw** a lion.

We use the past simple to talk about a _____ activity in the past.
We use the past continuous to talk about a _____ activity in the past.

2 What's the difference between these sentences?

When she arrived I made some coffee.
When she arrived I was making some coffee.

3 Do you have the same rules in your language?

Practice

> The most common verbs in written English are almost the same, but *mean*, *like*, *put*, and *let* aren't in the top 20, and *work*, *find*, *help*, and *ask* are.

1 ▣1 You will hear the twenty most common verbs in spoken English (most of them are irregular). What is the past tense of each verb?

2 The *-ed* ending of regular verbs can be pronounced in three ways.

1 Put these verbs from the text into the correct column.

| decided | ended | stopped | refused |
| started | arrived | celebrated | finished |

/ɪd/	/d/	/t/	

2 Can you add two more verbs to each column?

3 Make sentences about Nick's journey using these words.

- a cobra
- elephants
- Cape Town
- 21 January

- the Egyptian military
- malaria
- birthday
- 3.30 a.m.

- chocolate cake
- 15
- bees
- cereal

4 **Against the clock** [3 minutes] Make as many sentences as you can.

I was travelling in Kenya when

I met my future husband.
I lost my passport.

1	travel / Kenya	slip / fall
2	wait / train	lose / passport
3	drive / airport	see / shark
4	climb / mountain	begin / feel ill
5	walk / Scotland	meet / future husband / wife
6	lie / beach	notice / not have / tickets
7	eat / cheap restaurant	fall asleep / get sunburnt
8	swim / Indian Ocean	someone / steal / wallet

5 **In pairs.** Ask and answer questions.
What were you doing when you met your future husband?

Can you remember ...?
- three things that happened to Nick Bourne
- ten common irregular verbs
- how to pronounce *-ed* endings

Practice p.86

Speak out

1 Complete the questions in this dialogue.

A I got back from my holiday last week.

B Where _____ ?

A Peru.

B Really? What _____ ?

A It was fantastic, really great.

B How long _____ ?

A Three weeks altogether – I wanted to stay longer!

B _____ expensive?

A Well, the flight was, but it was cheap when we got there.

B Who _____ ?

A My sister and her boyfriend.

B _____ any problems?

A Nothing serious. I lost my watch.

B How _____ happen?

A We were staying in a cheap hotel and I left it in the bathroom.

B _____ go back?

A Yes, I'd love to. Maybe next year ...

2 **In pairs.** Talk about your last holiday. Use the questions above, and try to find out as much as you can.

06
ON THE ROAD

In this lesson

- Transport vocabulary
- Asking for travel information
- Making hotel bookings

Speak for yourself

1 Look at these pictures. Which do you think look ...?

- most exciting
- most comfortable
- most interesting

2 Which would / wouldn't you like to experience when travelling? Compare your ideas.

Vocabulary

Transport

 1 Listen. Where would you hear these announcements?

2 Can you think of more forms of transport?

3 Which can you get off? get on? get into? get out of? ride?

4 Make word webs for some of the forms of transport. Include places, people, and verbs.

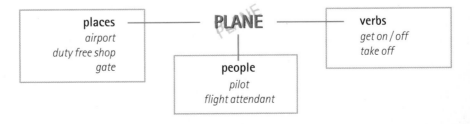

places	PLANE	verbs
airport		*get on / off*
duty free shop		*take off*
gate		
	people	
	pilot	
	flight attendant	

English in use
Travel situations

1 You're going to hear two dialogues. Think of two questions you expect to hear in each one.
- asking for train information
- booking a hotel room

2 Look at these sentences.

    1 A _____ ?

       B A double, please, ensuite if possible.

    2 Single or return?

    3 First or standard?

    4 A _____ ?

       B Yes, a continental breakfast.

    5 A _____ ?

       B Sunday, about 10 o'clock.

    1 Which dialogues are they from?

    2 Can you complete the questions?

Asking for travel information

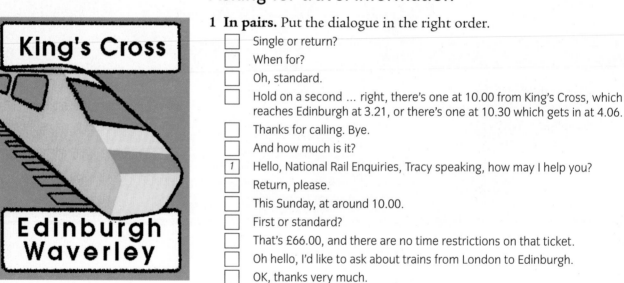

1 **In pairs.** Put the dialogue in the right order.

- [ ] Single or return?
- [ ] When for?
- [ ] Oh, standard.
- [ ] Hold on a second … right, there's one at 10.00 from King's Cross, which reaches Edinburgh at 3.21, or there's one at 10.30 which gets in at 4.06.
- [ ] Thanks for calling. Bye.
- [ ] And how much is it?
- [1] Hello, National Rail Enquiries, Tracy speaking, how may I help you?
- [ ] Return, please.
- [ ] This Sunday, at around 10.00.
- [ ] First or standard?
- [ ] That's £66.00, and there are no time restrictions on that ticket.
- [ ] Oh hello, I'd like to ask about trains from London to Edinburgh.
- [ ] OK, thanks very much.

 2 Join another pair and compare your answers.

    1 Do you agree on the order?

    2 Listen and check your ideas.

3 Imagine you want to fly from London to your home town. Change the dialogue as necessary.

A Hello, Eurotravel, how may I help you?

B Hello, I'd like to ask …

> Before you ask for travel information prepare your questions, and think about the questions you will need to answer.

Booking a hotel room

1 Try to complete the dialogue.

Receptionist	Good evening madam, how can I help you?
Guest	
Receptionist	One moment, I'll just check.
Guest	
Receptionist	How many nights would you like to stay?
Guest	
Receptionist	Would you like a single, a double, or a twin?
Guest	
Receptionist	Yes, we have a double ensuite deluxe.
Guest	
Receptionist	For the two nights that's £250.
Guest	
Receptionist	Yes, a continental breakfast.
Guest	
Receptionist	Very good. Could you fill in this card, please?

Can you remember ...?

- eight forms of transport
- three types of hotel room
- four questions a travel agent would ask

Practice p.87

 2 Listen. Is your dialogue the same? Check in Tapescript 6.3 on *p.106*.

3 **In pairs.** Make another hotel dialogue, changing the details above.

Useful language

1 Look at the expressions and mark them **T** for travel information and **H** for hotel.

I'd like	to ask about trains from _____ to _____ .
	to ask about flights from _____ to _____ .
	a double room, please.

| When | would you like | to travel? |
| How many nights | | to stay? |

Would you like	first or economy?
	a single or a return?
	a single, a double, or a twin?

| Could you | fill in this card? |
| | tell me how much a return costs? |

2 ◎4 Listen to these questions.
1 Does the intonation rise or fall at the end?
2 Practise the questions.

3 If you were speaking English, which situation would you feel most confident in?

Speak out

1 **In pairs.** Choose 'travel information' or 'booking a hotel room'. Underline appropriate words and information below, and make dialogues.

single / return   first / standard   Saturday morning
how many nights?
flights   New York   London 7.50 / Bristol 9.25
breakfast   single / double / twin   London to Bristol £320
fill in   Tuesday, 8.00 a.m.   first / economy
£24.50   £85   London 8.15 / Bristol 9.35   trains   free rooms

2 Practise your dialogue and perform it for the class.

07
ENJOY YOUR TRIP!

In this lesson

- Travel vocabulary
- Multi-word verbs
- Planning what to take on holiday

Speak for yourself

1 Here are some things that people always take with them when they travel, and their reasons for taking them. Match the 'travel essentials' to the reasons.

1 I never leave without a moisturiser.
2 We always take a travel alarm clock.
3 My essential is a corkscrew.
4 I never leave without my cassette recorder.
5 I make sure I take travel sickness pills.
6 I wouldn't travel without earplugs.
7 Our essential is a short-wave radio.

a We often have to get up at dawn to catch flights.
b We can keep in touch with things back home.
c I record my feelings, and listening to the tape brings back more memories than a diary.
d Long flights, hot sunshine, and hotel air conditioning really dry out my skin.
e They're great for getting to sleep in noisy hotel rooms.
f I'm a hopeless traveller – I get carsick, airsick, and seasick.
g I was once delayed at an airport in Bulgaria, and the only thing I had to drink was a bottle of wine.

2 What are your 'travel essentials'? Why?

Vocabulary
Packing your bags

1 The extracts below are from guidebooks for Iceland and Zimbabwe. Read the extracts and match them to the countries.

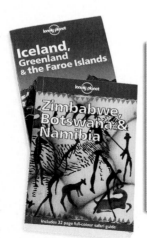

There are three things that no traveller here should be without: a tent, a sleeping bag, and a torch. Take a tracksuit for mornings and evenings in game parks, with shorts for the daytime. A jacket and warm socks are a good idea as it can get cold at night. Other items which will be handy are a small travel alarm, a basic first aid kit, a water bottle, a towel, a camera and film, a penknife, and any batteries that you need. Take insect repellent, suncream, and a money belt. **1**

Warm clothing will be of great importance to everyone. Between May and September you should take several pairs of thick socks, heavy windproof gloves, high-protection sunglasses, a wool hat, a jumper, hiking shorts, wool shirt and trousers (jeans are cold and uncomfortable when wet), and a waterproof jacket. Travellers in winter need to prepare for Arctic conditions. If you're camping, take your own stove, and as much dried food as possible. **2**

2 Imagine you're going to one of these countries. How many things have you got already, and what would you have to buy?

Practice

1 When you last packed a bag, where were you going and what exactly did you take? Make a list.

2 **Against the clock** `3 minutes` **In pairs. A** asks 'Why did you take _____ ?' and **B** answers. Then change over.

   A *Why did you take a penknife?*

   B *Because it's useful for peeling fruit. Why did you take a torch?*

3 There are lots of compound nouns in the texts, like *sleeping bag*.

   1 How many can you make from these words?

insect	cream	belt	sun	water
knife	pen	repellent	money	bottle
travel	glasses	alarm		

   2 Where is the stress in words like this? Practise saying them.

Multi-word verbs   Extra!

a 🔲1 Listen to these seven dialogues. Are they before, during, or after the holiday?

b Listen again and write exactly what the second person says.

c Underline the multi-word verbs in the sentences. Check the meaning.

d Can you remember the first lines? Work in pairs and practise the dialogues.

Can you remember ...?

• eight things to take to Zimbabwe

• three multi-word verbs

• how compound nouns are pronounced

Practice p.88

Speak out

1 **In groups.** Choose one of these trips.

   • Norway for an adventure holiday.

   • Florida on a business trip.

   • Spain for a sightseeing holiday.

2 What sort of bag would you take and what would you pack? Why? Choose from the items below and add more of your own.

camera and film
cosmetics
driving licence
beach towel
sandals
traveller's cheques
mosquito repellent
passport
phrase book
walking boots
guidebook
T-shirts
diary
novels
jeans
suit and tie
jumper
sunglasses
raincoat
shorts

In this lesson

- Travel advice
- Listening: a holiday incident
- Describing a holiday problem

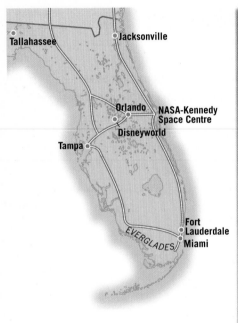

Listen for yourself
Foreign Office advice

1 What do you know about Florida? Would you like to go there on holiday? Why / Why not?

2 In pairs. Complete this advice for visitors to Florida.

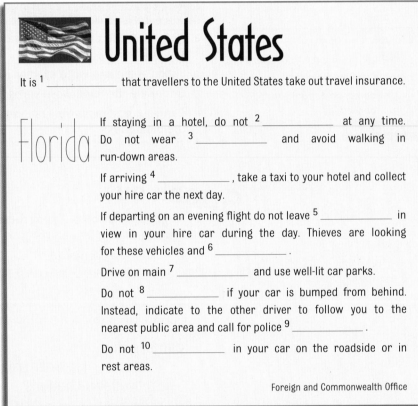

United States

It is ¹ _____ that travellers to the United States take out travel insurance.

Florida

If staying in a hotel, do not ² _____ at any time. Do not wear ³ _____ and avoid walking in run-down areas.

If arriving ⁴ _____ , take a taxi to your hotel and collect your hire car the next day.

If departing on an evening flight do not leave ⁵ _____ in view in your hire car during the day. Thieves are looking for these vehicles and ⁶ _____ .

Drive on main ⁷ _____ and use well-lit car parks.

Do not ⁸ _____ if your car is bumped from behind. Instead, indicate to the other driver to follow you to the nearest public area and call for police ⁹ _____ .

Do not ¹⁰ _____ in your car on the roadside or in rest areas.

Foreign and Commonwealth Office

3 🔲 Listen to someone calling the Foreign Office travel advice line.

1 How many countries have recorded information?
2 Check your ideas about visiting Florida.

4 🔲 Listen to these three sentences again. Which words are stressed?

> When you listen to spoken English you need to understand the important words. These are usually stressed.

Listen 2
Highway robbery!

○3

1 Listen to four sentences about a holiday in Florida. Complete the gaps.

1 _____ _____ in the twenty-first century!

2 It all happened _____ _____ _____ _____ .

3 I didn't really know _____ _____ _____ .

4 I _____ _____ _____ and so did he.

2 What do you think happened? Which piece of Foreign Office advice did they ignore?

○4

3 Now listen to the whole story. Were you right?

> What's the difference between *rob* and *steal*?

4 Listen again. Are these sentences true (✔) or false (✗)?

1 The whole family enjoyed the holiday.

2 They didn't have any problems until the end.

3 Chris was driving a hire car.

4 The robbers were violent.

5 The robbers took everything.

6 Nobody was hurt.

7 Chris and his family missed their flight.

8 The police didn't help.

5 Against the clock 2 minutes Put these sentences in the order they were used in the story.

	One of them had a baseball bat.
1	The kids had a great time.
	It didn't take long for the police to arrive.
	I was pretty angry, I can tell you.
	The luggage, our coats, even the spare tyre.
	We were driving to the airport.
	Suddenly a big car bumped into the back of us.
	They didn't take our souvenirs.

> **Did you notice ...?**
> - a phrase which means *You aren't serious.*
> - a difference between British and American vocabulary
>
> Check in Tapescript 8.4.
>
> Practice *p.89*

6 In pairs. Practise telling the story. Use the sentences above. Include as much detail as you can.

Speak out

1 You are going to talk about a problem that you or someone you know has had on holiday.

1 Think about these things.
- What happened?
- Who did it happen to?
- When did it happen?
- Where did it happen?

2 Write down ten words you're going to use to tell your story.

2 In groups. Tell your stories. Ask more questions.

09
BEING IN TOUCH

In this lesson

- Present perfect and past simple
- Past participles
- Giving news

Speak for yourself

Find out if these statements are true (✓) or false (✗) by doing a class survey. If they are false, change them so that they are true.

1 Some of us have sent a fax recently.
2 A few of us have written an e-mail this week.
3 Most of us write letters regularly.
4 We all send birthday cards to family and friends.
5 One of us has received a postcard recently.
6 Nobody has ever used a videophone.
7 A lot of us made more than ten phone calls last week.

Grammar

Present perfect and past simple

1 Read these messages. Decide if they are from an answerphone, an e-mail, a letter, or a postcard. How do you know?

1 Sorry I haven't been in touch this week, but I've had a lot of problems to sort out at work. Anyway, now you've got e-mail I thought I'd drop you a line. Have you _____ Mike this week?

2 Hello, Vic? It's Silvana here. I'm off to Italy next week. Have you ever _____ to Rome? Do you know any good hotels? Can you call me back? Thanks!

3 Dear Pete, How are you? I haven't seen you for months! I hope you're settling into your new house. Have you _____ a new cooker?

4 As you can see I'm on a skiing holiday! I've never seen such beautiful mountains, but I'm afraid I'll break my leg or something! I've _____ hundreds of photos.

5 My computer crashed last week, so I couldn't answer your message. Work's been terrible this week – my boss has _____ me to work this weekend.

6 Hi Jan, it's me. I'm ringing to ask if you've _____ to Paul. Do you know where he is? Call me when you can!

7 Having a fantastic time. The weather's not too bad. This week we've _____ three sunny days, but yesterday wasn't very nice, so we went to a museum. Wish you were here!

8 I can't remember what number your house is, so I hope this arrives. How have you been? I've had an exciting time since Christmas – three trips abroad. In January I went to Brazil, and this month I've _____ to Paris three times.

2 Complete the gaps in the messages. Compare your ideas with a partner. What verbs did you use?

3 Look at these sentences from the texts.

a This week we've had three sunny days.

   Sorry I haven't been in touch this week.

   Have you ever been to Rome?

b My computer crashed last week.

   Yesterday wasn't very nice.

   In January I went to Brazil.

1 What tense is used in the sentences in **a**?

2 What tense is used in the sentences in **b**?

Present perfect and past simple

Form

Complete this rule and the table.

We make the present perfect with h _____ or h _____ and a _____ participle.

+	–	?
I've seen Paul today.	I _____ Paul today.	_____ you _____ Paul today?
He's been to Madrid.	He _____ to Madrid.	_____ he _____ to Madrid?

Use

1 Look at the examples. Complete the rules with *finished* or *unfinished*.

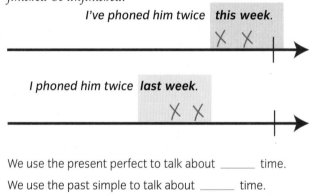

I've phoned him twice **this week**.

I phoned him twice **last week**.

We use the present perfect to talk about _____ time.

We use the past simple to talk about _____ time.

2 Compare the rules for the present perfect and the past simple with your language. Are they the same or different?

3 **In pairs.** Correct the mistakes in these sentences (there may be more than one possible correction).

1 I've written two letters yesterday.

2 Do you have been to Holland?

3 She phoned me four times this week.

4 He haven't lived here for long.

5 They've been to France ten years ago.

6 Never I haven't broke my leg.

7 We've had breakfast two hours ago.

8 I've worked there until 1997.

Practice

1 Listen. What happens to *have* and *has*? What happens to *been*?

John's gone on holiday.

Work's been terrible.

I haven't seen you for ages.

Have you ever been to the States?

How many books have you read?

2 Copy the stress and intonation. Try to sound exactly the same.

3 Against the clock `2 minutes` What are the past participles of these verbs?

ride	write	be	meet	break
see	sing	speak	live	eat
understand	give	win	forget	buy
come	teach	make	ring	send

4 In pairs. Give your partner a number and a letter. Your partner makes a sentence in the present perfect or the past simple.

A 1, f
B She didn't phone me last week.

1	She / not phone me	a	this year
2	It / very wet	b	this month
3	I / not see him	c	last October
4	We / go to London	d	yesterday
5	They / not eat out	e	this week
6	I / write two letters	f	last week

5 Match verbs in exercise 3 with these things.

forget – your mother's birthday

- your mother's birthday
- in an expensive restaurant
- a sunrise from a mountaintop
- your leg
- abroad
- a politician
- a motorbike
- to a newspaper
- in public
- dinner for more than three people

6 In groups. Ask questions with *Have you ever …?* Ask more questions with the past simple – find out as much as you can.

Have you ever forgotten your mother's birthday?
What did she say? What did you do?

Speak out

1 Imagine you meet a friend that you haven't seen for six months. Tell him / her what you've done, and ask questions about what he / she's done. Think about these things.

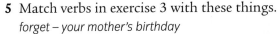

work holidays THINGS YOU'VE BOUGHT
relationships

2 Start your conversation like this.

A Hello! I haven't seen you for ages! How are you?
B I'm fine. It's been a busy few months.
A Why? What's happened?
B Well, …

REPEAT!
MORE SLOWLY!
AGAIN, PLEASE!
SPEAK UP!
PLEASE SPELL!

Speak for yourself

1 **In groups.** Have you ever made a phone call in English? Who to? Did you have any problems?

2 Complete this statement in as many ways as possible.
   Phone calls in English can be difficult because ...

3 Look at the picture. What problems is this student of English having?

4 Make the student sound more polite and friendly. Put these words in the right order to make useful sentences.
   1 say   you   that   you   ,   couldn't   again   could   ?
   2 I'm   you   I   quite   hear   ,   can't   sorry
   3 please   up   could   ,   bit   speak   you   a   ?
   4 that   do   spell   how   you   ?
   5 I'm   quite   catch   ,   didn't   I   sorry   that
   6 bit   ,   speak   slowly   you   could   please   a   more   ?

 5 Listen and check. Practise saying the sentences.

Vocabulary

Telephones

1 Match the verbs with the nouns.

1	pick	a message
2	answer	a number
3	make	the phone down
4	ring	someone up
5	put	the phone up
6	leave	the line
7	dial	the phone
8	hold	a call

 2 Listen and decide what to do (you can sometimes do more than one thing).

- put the phone down / hang up
- answer the phone
- try again later
- hold on / hold the line
- dial an extension number
- dial a single number
- redial with a new number
- leave a message
- check you have the right number

Do you know what these phone numbers are for in Britain?

999   192   1471   100   155

English in use

On the phone

1 In pairs. Read the phone dialogue below and try to number the boxes in the right order.

- [ ] I'm sorry, he's engaged at the moment. Will you hold?
- [ ] Could you tell him Allan called?
- [ ] Allan MacFarlane.
- [ ] Thank you.
- [1] International Shipping, Elaine speaking, how may I help you?
- [ ] Hold on a moment please, Mr MacFarlane.
- [ ] Thanks very much. Goodbye.
- [ ] Could I speak to Bob Harris, please?
- [ ] No, thanks, I'll ring back later.
- [ ] Could I ask who's calling?
- [ ] Would you like to leave a message?
- [ ] Certainly Mr MacFarlane, I'll tell him.

 2 Listen and check.

3 Listen again. What's different?

4 Listen to a different call. Write exactly what you hear. Check your ideas in Tapescript 10.5 on *p.107.*

A Hello?

B Hello. _____ , please?

A Who _____ ?

B _____ Mark.

A Hello, Mark. _____ , I'll just _____ .
I think she's _____ . She'll _____ .

B OK, _____ . I'll _____ .

A Can I _____ ?

B Just tell her _____ .

A OK. _____ .

B _____ .

On the telephone say who you are like this:
It's (Tom) not *I'm (Tom)*.

5 Listen to these questions. Does the intonation rise or fall at the end?

1 Can I speak to Mike, please?

2 Who is it?

3 Could I leave a message?

4 Would you like to leave a message?

5 Can you ring back later?

6 Practise the questions. Try to sound exactly the same.

Useful language

1 Complete the gaps with words and phrases.

Formal	Informal	
Could I speak to the manager, please?	_____ to John, please? / Is John _____ , please?	C
_____ I _____ who's calling?	Who's _____ ? / Who _____ it?	
Hold _____ a moment, please.	_____ on a _____ .	
I'll just _____ you through.	I'll just _____ her.	
_____ I leave a message?	_____ ?	
_____ to _____ a message?	Can I _____ her a _____ ?	
_____ you _____ her I called?	Just _____ him I _____ .	
I'll ring / phone _____ later. *(formal and informal)*		
Goodbye.	_____ .	

2 Mark the sentences **C** for the caller and **A** for the person answering.

3 Which phrases do you think you would use most often? Which wouldn't you use? Why?

Speak out

1 **In pairs.** Look at the conversations below. Decide what to say, then have the conversations.

A	B	A	B
Network Systems / speaking / help you?	speak / Helen Potter?	hello?	speak / Julian?
who / calling?	name	who?	name
hold / moment	thank	hang / second	OK
sorry / engaged / hold?	no / ring back	gone out	ring back
leave / message?	called	leave / message?	called
certainly	thank / goodbye	OK	thank / bye
goodbye		bye	

Can you remember …?
- five expressions you would use or hear on the telephone
- five 'telephone' verbs
- three useful phone numbers in Britain

Practice p.91

2 Now change the dialogues and have formal and informal dialogues of your own.

3 Perform your dialogues for the class.

It's for you…

11
TALK TO ME

Speak for yourself

1 Think of one advantage and one disadvantage of each of these things.
- mobile phones
- the Internet
- laptops
- fax machines
- satellite television
- answering machines

2 Does new technology improve people's lives? Why / Why not?

Vocabulary

Technology and communication

1 These texts are about three different ways of communicating. What is each text referring to? Is it 'for' or 'against'?

2 Which points of view do you agree with?

1 There's no escape. They seem to be ringing everywhere these days. Nowhere is safe – restaurants, trains, pubs, even cinemas and theatres. People never turn them off, and listening to other people's conversations drives me mad.

2 A recent US survey found that managers often receive over 200 messages a day. Many office workers switch off their computers so they can get some work done ...

3 Lots of people don't often need to use them. But imagine you're driving along in the middle of nowhere and you break down. You can phone for help straight away, and save time, money, and worry.

4 Surfing the net is becoming a major free-time activity for millions of people. The problem? 99% of what's on it is rubbish. Some people say it will replace books, newspapers, and magazines, but I don't think so.

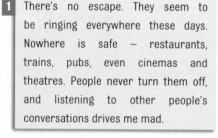

5 All human knowledge is there. Want to know about French literature, the US Space Programme, the love life of frogs? Just log on and learn. It's like being in the world's biggest library, but with no librarians.

6 It's fantastic, it's so convenient. I can switch on my computer, press a button, send a document, and seconds later someone can open it on the other side of the world. I never use snail mail anymore!

3 Make short statements for and against satellite television. Try to use these words and phrases.

channels	sports	wonderful	whenever you want
rubbish	programmes	quality	whatever you want
quiz shows	awful	choice	24 hours a day

Practice

1 Cover the texts. Complete these phrases.

1 People never t _____ their mobile phones o _____ .

2 S _____ the net is a major free-time activity.

3 Managers often r _____ over 200 e-mails a day.

4 Just l _____ o _____ and learn.

5 You can p _____ for help wherever you are.

6 I can s _____ o _____ my computer, s _____ a document round the world, and someone can o _____ it a few minutes later.

2 Check the meaning of these verbs. How many opposites to the verbs above can you find?

turn on	turn up	turn down	watch
plug in	write	unplug	switch off
close	log off	listen to	read

3 **In pairs.** Complete the word web with verbs from exercises 1 and 2.

4 🔘 Listen and write down these e-mail addresses and websites. Check in Tapescript 11.1 on *p.107.* Practise saying them.

Similar words   *Extra!*

a Put these words into three groups.

see	hear	speak
listen to	talk	look at
say	watch	tell

b **In pairs.** Correct the mistakes in these sentences.

1 He said me his name.

2 Ssh! I'm hearing the news.

3 Hello? Hello? I can't listen to you.

4 What did he say you?

5 I looked at the TV for three hours last night.

6 It's completely black – I can't look at anything.

---

computer
turn on / off

radio
turn up / down

COMMUNICATION

TV

letter / e-mail

Check that you remember how to say the alphabet – you often have to spell these addresses.

Can you remember ...?

• four ways of communicating

• how to say e-mail addresses and websites

• four 'television' verbs

Practice p.91

Speak out

1 What do you think? Delete the coloured words to make sentences.

1 I ~~never~~ use a computer ~~when I have to~~ every day.

2 I would never happily use a mobile phone only in emergencies.

3 I think e-mails are better worse than letters.

4 I'd find a laptop very useful useful once in a while useless.

5 Having an answering machine is isn't important to me.

6 I've got haven't got will never have a satellite television.

7 I never occasionally use the Internet a lot.

8 Books and newspapers will never soon be replaced.

2 **In groups.** Compare your answers, and explain them. Who is the most 'techno-friendly' person?

12
OUT OF TOUCH

In this lesson

- Agreeing and disagreeing
- Listening: male and female English
- Talking about men and women

Listen for yourself
What do you think?

1 In groups. Do you think a man or a woman would say these things? Why? What could the situation be?

1 *Let me look at the map.*

2 How do I look?

3 **Come on! Hurry up!**

4 But you never do the washing up!

5 **Where did I put the car keys?**

6 Do you want to talk about it?

7 We never go out any more.

8 *I love you, too.*

9 **You're wearing a new shirt!**

10 *I'll do it later.*

 2 Listen to two people discussing 1–10 above. Do they have the same ideas as you?

3 Look at these phrases.

That's what I think.	I don't agree (with that).
That's true.	So do I.
Definitely not.	That's not true.
I agree (with that).	Neither do I.
That's rubbish.	I disagree (with that).
Definitely.	Me too.

1 Which are for agreeing? Which are for disagreeing?

2 Listen again. Tick (✓) the phrases the people use.

4 Think of three more things that men or women typically say. Compare your ideas.

Listen 2

His and Her English

1 Complete these statements with *men, women, male,* or *female*.

1 _____ change their minds more often than _____ .

2 The _____ mosquito is the one which bites.

3 _____ describe colours better than _____ .

4 _____ have better memories than _____ .

5 _____ apologize more than _____ .

6 _____ talk more than _____ .

7 _____ talk more about jobs, _____ talk more about emotions.

8 _____ are more polite.

9 _____ birds are usually more colourful than _____ birds.

10 _____ are safer drivers than _____ .

2 In pairs. Compare your ideas. Do you agree?

3 Read this information about a radio programme.

1 Listen and check your answers to exercise 1.

2 Which sentences are not discussed?

4 Against the clock 3 minutes What can you remember?

1 Complete this table about men's and women's speech.

linguistic differences	topic differences

2 Listen again. Check your ideas.

> 10.30–10.45 **Morning Thoughts** looks at speech, and how women's is different from men's. Is it how they talk, or what they talk about?

Did you notice ...?

verbs which mean
to say sorry
to have a friendly conversation
to talk about other people
to say that you aren't satisfied

Check in Tapescript 12.2.

Practice p.92

Speak out

Are you a typical woman or man?

1 Think of five ways that you're typical and five ways that you're not. Think about these things.

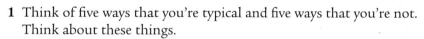

topics of conversation
books and magazines
working TV
eating socializing
clothes and hair

2 In groups. Compare your ideas. Who is most 'typical', and who is most 'different'?

13
BEING A CONSUMER

In this lesson

- Money vocabulary
- First conditional, *when*, *before*, *after*, *as soon as*
- Discussing ideas for saving money

Speak for yourself

1 Think of three things that you spend your money on
- every day.
- every week.
- once a month.
- once a year.

2 Compare with a partner. Do you spend your money on the same things?

Vocabulary

Money

1 Match these words with the pictures.

credit card	wallet	cheques	purse
coins	notes	traveller's cheques	

2 Check the meaning of the verbs below and complete the questions.

afford	spend	save	buy
pay for	cost	lend	borrow

1 Do you try to _____ money or do you usually _____ it as soon as you get it?

2 Do you _____ your shopping in cash or by credit card?

3 How much does a CD _____ where you live?

4 What kinds of thing do you _____ second-hand?

5 Do you ever _____ money or _____ money to other people? What for? Who to?

6 What can't you _____ to do this year?

3 **In pairs.** Ask and answer the questions.

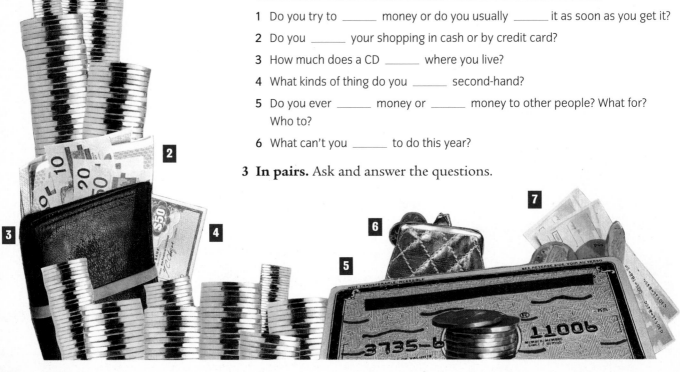

Grammar
First conditional

1 Read this advertisement. Which parts do you believe? Would you try it?

Can you survive abroad?

If you go abroad this year, how will you communicate? What will you say when you order food and drink in a restaurant, or if you need a receipt? How will you ask for travel information, change traveller's cheques, or understand taxi drivers? If you can speak the language, you'll enjoy your holiday or business trip much more. People will be friendlier, and you'll save money and have a better time. But if you can't speak the language, you'll never survive.

Anyone can learn a language in three weeks!

We guarantee that if you study for just three weeks before you go, you'll be able to say whatever you need to. You'll start learning as soon as you open your book.

All you need to do is turn on the cassette player, read, listen, and repeat. If you study for ten minutes every day, you'll soon have a vocabulary of over 300 words for everyday situations.

Yes! You can afford it

The course costs just £29.99, and if you order in the next ten days you'll save £5.00.

Our promise

Of course, if you're not completely satisfied we'll refund your money. But we think you'll enjoy learning a language so much that you'll want to keep studying after you get back home!

2 In pairs. Cover the text and complete these sentences.

1 People will be friendlier if …
2 How will you communicate if …?
3 We'll refund your money if …
4 If you study for three weeks before …
5 As soon as you open your book …
6 We think that after you get home …
7 You'll save £5.00 if …
8 You won't survive if …

3 Do we use *will* or the present simple after *if, when, before, after,* and *as soon as*?

First conditional

Form

Choose the correct verb forms to make example sentences.

+ *If she studies / 'll study for three weeks, she'll speak perfect Italian.*

− *If I won't study / don't study every day, I won't learn anything.*

? *How will / do they ask for a receipt if they don't speak Russian?*

Use

1 We use the first conditional to talk about *possible* events in the future. What's the difference between these sentences?
I'll tell him if I see him.
I'll tell him when I see him.

2 We also use the present simple to talk about the future after *when, before, after,* and *as soon as.* Find as many examples as you can in the advert.

Practice

The future of *can / can't* is *will / won't be able to*.
Find an example in the advert on *p.35*.

1 Richard wants to borrow £5,000 to buy a car. What does he say to his bank manager? What does his bank manager think? Make sentences with *If*...

If you lend me £5,000, I'll buy a car.

If I buy a car ...

If you lend me £5,000,
⬇
I / buy a car
⬇
I / not travel by train
⬇
I / not spend money on tickets
⬇
I / save £300 a month
⬇
I / open another bank account
⬇
I / save more money
⬇
you / be happy

If I lend him £5,000,
⬇
he / buy a car
⬇
he / have to pay for petrol and insurance
⬇
he / not have much money
⬇
he / not be able to pay back the loan
⬇
he / sell the car
⬇
he / get less than he paid
⬇
I / lose money

2 In pairs. Test each other. Ask questions about Richard.

What will happen if he ...?

3 Against the clock `3 minutes` Make as many sentences as you can about your life with *if* or *when* (they can be negative sentences too).

If I get married, I'll ...

When I get a degree I'll ...

get married	get a degree	have children
change my job	buy a big house	have enough money
make a lot of money	retire early	start my own business
meet the man / woman of my dreams		

Can you remember ...?

• six 'money' verbs

• three advantages of speaking the language when you travel

• how to form the first conditional

Practice p.92

Speak out

1 Look at these ideas about how to save money. What are the good and bad points of each idea?

If you pay off your credit card, you won't have to pay interest, but credit cards are very convenient.

• Pay off your credit card. You often have to pay interest on what you borrow – about 20% a year. Then cut your card up and throw it away!

• If you use public transport, you won't have to buy petrol and pay for insurance.

• Move to a smaller house or flat. Your bills will be much lower.

• Don't go away on holiday. If you go abroad, you'll spend a fortune on flights, hotels, and food. If you stay at home, you'll save all that money.

• Don't cook special dinners for friends. If they're really your friends, they won't mind what you give them to eat.

2 Can you think of any more ideas for saving money?

Speak for yourself

1 Complete these sentences about food in Britain. Compare your ideas.

1 A typical breakfast is _____ .

2 The main meal of the day is _____ .

3 Dinner is usually eaten between _____ and _____ p.m.

4 A lot of office workers have _____ for lunch.

5 The national dish is _____ .

6 The national drink is _____ .

7 People eat _____ nearly every day.

8 _____ and Indian restaurants are very popular.

2 Now write sentences about your country.

Vocabulary

Restaurants

 1 Against the clock 3 minutes Which words go with each picture?

menu	tablecloth	straw	waiter
ketchup	wine glass	candles	salt and pepper
tray	milkshake	cutlery	wine list
paper napkin	flowers	French fries	bin
plastic cup	tip	bill	fast food

2 When would you eat in restaurants like this? Who with?

English in use
Eating in and out

 1 Listen and write the sentences you hear.

2 Match these questions with the sentences. Are the dialogues in a restaurant or café, or in someone's house? How do you know?

a How would you like the steak?

b Do you want some more ice-cream?

c Shall I lay the table for you?

d How much is that?

e Would you like to see the wine list?

f Would you like anything else?

g Could we have the bill, please?

h Could you pass the salt, please?

3 In pairs. Put this restaurant dialogue in the right order.

☐	I'll have the vegetable soup to start …
1	Are you ready to order, sir?
☐	The salmon with a salad.
☐	I'll have the vegetable soup too, please.
☐	And I'll have a steak, I think.
☐	Two vegetable soups.
☐	Yes, I think so. Darling?
☐	Thank you very much, sir. Would you like to see the wine list?
☐	And for you, sir?
☐	How would you like it, sir? Rare, medium, or well done?
☐	The vegetable soup. And to follow, madam?
☐	Very rare – blue if you can.

Starters

Grilled sardines
Vegetable soup
Melon and Parma ham
Thai salad

Main courses
Grilled salmon
Fillet steak
(served with vegetables or a salad)
Chicken curry with rice
Vegetarian lasagne

 4 Listen and check your ideas.

5 In groups. Practise the dialogue. Then close the book and see if you can remember it.

6 Change roles and perform the dialogue again. You can change the things you order if you want.

Useful language

Complete the boxes with these words.

Waiter   Host   Customer   Guest

Restaurant

1 [____]	Are you ready to order?
2 [____] Could I have	the tomato soup? some more bread? the bill, please?
3 [____] Would you like	to see the wine list? ice and lemon?
4 [____] I'll have / I'd like	a salad, please. a glass of mineral water.

Someone's house

5 [____] Would you like	a second helping? some more bread? milk and sugar?

Could you pass the salt, please?

6 [____] This is really delicious.

No, thanks, it was lovely but I can't manage any more.

Grammar

Short questions

> We often don't use full questions e.g. we can say *Would you like tea or coffee?* or *Tea or coffee?*

1 Complete these pairs. What are the questions about?

1 Black or w _____ ?

2 M _____ and sugar?

3 With or _____ sugar?

4 Brown or _____ bread?

5 Red or w _____ ?

6 English or c _____ breakfast?

7 Ice and l _____ ?

8 Still or s _____ ?

 2 Listen to this pattern. Repeat the questions. Try to sound exactly the same.

Would you like some toast?

Like some toast?

Some toast?

Toast?

3 Practise the pattern with these words.

| pepper | coffee | orange juice | tea |

4 **In pairs.** Look at this dialogue. Take out as many words as you can.

Waiter	Are you ready to order?	*Ready to order?*
Customer	Yes, I'd like to have the potato soup.	
Waiter	Would you like white or brown bread?	
Customer	I'd like some white bread, please.	
Waiter	And what would you like to follow?	
Customer	I'd just like a chicken salad, please.	
Waiter	And what would you like to drink?	
Customer	I'll have a glass of mineral water.	
Waiter	Would you like still or sparkling?	
Customer	I'd like sparkling, please.	
Waiter	Would you like ice and lemon?	
Customer	I'd like both, please.	

> **Can you remember ...?**
> - five words you associate with fast food
> - four questions you would ask or answer in a restaurant
>
> **Practice p.93**

 5 Listen and check your ideas. Then practise the dialogue.

Speak out

In pairs. Tell each other about your favourite restaurant.

Where is it?

What kind of restaurant is it?

What's it like?

What food and drink can you have there?

Who do you go there with?

Is it expensive?

15
FOOD TO GO

In this lesson
- Supermarket vocabulary
- Countable and uncountable nouns
- Describing a perfect meal

Speak for yourself

1 What supermarkets do you have in your country? Are there any differences between them?

2 These products are all for sale in supermarkets. Look at the labels. What do you think they are?

1 **Perfect with red meat, pasta, and cheeses.**
Open one hour before serving.
Serve between 16–18°C.

2 **Wash before eating**

3 Take two every four hours.

4 **Avoid contact with eyes and skin.**
Do not drink.
Keep out of reach of children.

5 Just add milk and sugar for a delicious start to the day

6 *So gentle you can wash your hair every day.*

7 Use one bag per cup.
Allow to stand for two minutes before removing bag.
Best served with milk.

8 **Once opened keep refrigerated**

Vocabulary
Supermarkets

1 This is a guide to a reorganized supermarket. Which things are better than before, and which are completely new?

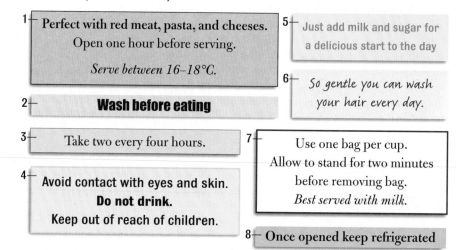

Your guide to a fresh new supermarket

Dear shopper
This simple guide is to tell you about the changes we have made.
You'll find lots of fresh new features, including a **bakery**, a **Salad Bar** serving delicious crisp salads, 1 _____ .
There's also a **wider choice** of frozen food 2 _____ , and our fish and meat counters have been improved.
On top of all this, **wider aisles** and a **larger restaurant** 3 _____ will make your visit more enjoyable.

If you need any assistance in finding anything, please don't hesitate to ask 4 _____ , or alternatively help is always at hand at our Customer Services Desk. We hope you enjoy the improvements 5 _____ .

Yours sincerely

Brian Otter Store Manager

PS Remember to sign up for your Loyalty Card 6 _____ .

2 Put these phrases in the correct place in the text.

a a member of staff

b to give you a better selection

c and look forward to seeing you again very soon

d to pick up even bigger savings

e with more seating

f and a brand new Food-To-Go Counter

3 What would you find in these sections of a supermarket?

- bakery
- toiletries
- frozen food
- snacks

4 Look at the vocabulary below and match it to a container.

a packet of	crisps	beans
a bottle of	biscuits	orange juice
a tin of	tuna	Coke
a can of	milk	shampoo
a carton of	tissues	matches
a box of	beer	chocolates

What's the difference?
a can of Coke / a Coke can
a packet of crisps / a crisp packet

5 🔊1 Listen. What happens to *a* and *of*?

Countable and uncountable nouns   *Extra!*

a Delete *countable* or *uncountable* to make rules.

1 Countable / Uncountable nouns have no plural.

2 Countable / Uncountable nouns can be either singular or plural.

3 Countable / Uncountable nouns can take *a* or *an*.

4 Countable / Uncountable nouns can take a plural verb.

5 With countable / uncountable nouns use *much*.

6 With countable / uncountable nouns use *many*.

b Look at the words in this lesson. Find five countable and five uncountable nouns.

Can you remember ...?

- five containers
- how to pronounce *a* and *of*
- three differences between countable and uncountable nouns

Practice p.94

Speak out

1 What would you need to buy for a perfect meal? Give as much detail as you can.

For breakfast I'd need to buy some Colombian coffee, a carton of milk, and some sugar. I'd need a loaf of bread ...

2 **In groups.** Compare your ideas. Who has the most expensive taste?

16
SHOP TILL YOU DROP

In this lesson

- Discussing opening hours
- Listening: changing shopping habits
- Likes and dislikes

SHOP OPENING TIMES

	AM	PM
MON	9.00 - 1.00	2.00 - 5.30
TUE	9.00 - 1.00	2.00 - 5.30
WED	9.00 - 1.00	2.00 - 5.30
THURS	9.00 - 1.00	2.00 - 5.30
FRI	9.00 - 1.00	2.00 - 5.30
SAT	9.00 - 1.00	CLOSED
SUN	CLOSED	CLOSED

Listen for yourself
Opening hours

1 What time do these places open and close ...?
- in your country
- in Britain

banks	supermarkets	post offices	bars
restaurants	cafés	nightclubs	smaller shops

2 Do these opening hours suit you? Which would you change?

3 `○ 1` Listen to these people talking about opening hours in different countries. Complete the table.

	country	place mentioned	opening hours	opinion
Roger				
Teresa				
Anna				

Listen 2
Time to shop

1 **Against the clock** `3 minutes` How many differences can you think of between the shops in the pictures? Think about these things.

- opening hours
- convenience
- personal service
- speed
- price
- selection
- location

2 You're going to listen to a tape about changes in British opening hours.

1 What do you think the main message is?
- Opening hours haven't changed much.
- Opening hours have changed, but people still shop at the same times.
- Opening hours have changed, and people now shop at all hours of the day and night.

2 Listen and check.

3 Listen again. Are these sentences true (✓) or false (✗)?

1 Not many people shop in the evenings.
2 Some people didn't want Sunday opening.
3 Most supermarkets are open 24 hours a day.
4 Supermarkets are busy all night.
5 Sundays are still different from other days of the week.
6 The Internet won't change shopping habits.

4 **In pairs.** Complete this table. Check in Tapescript 16.2 on *p.108.*

	time	reason
woman 1	*the evening*	
man 1	7.00 – 8.00 p.m.	
woman 2		
young women		
man 2		

Did you notice ...?

the phrases people used to talk about what they like and don't like

How many can you find in Tapescript 16.2?

Practice p.94

Speak out

1 Complete this questionnaire.

Are you a shopaholic?

Mark these sentences true (✓) or false (✗).

1 I enjoy shopping for clothes.
2 I like buying Christmas presents.
3 I think shops should be open every day of the week.
4 Shopping is good family entertainment.
5 Shopping cheers me up.
6 I buy new clothes at least once a month.
7 I have two or more credit cards.
8 I love window shopping.
9 I often buy clothes and then never wear them.
10 I always buy something when I go shopping.

2 **In groups.** Compare your answers.

17
BEING A FOREIGNER

Oo	Ooo	oOo
busy		polluted

Speak for yourself

1 In pairs. What cities and countries are the people describing?

I imagine ancient mountains, cold winds, rain, hill farms, sheep, and dragons when I think of ... Wales.

1 I imagine very green hills, lots of cows, soft rain, folk music, and Guinness when I think of ...

2 I imagine an enormous island, a beautiful coastline, a dry desert interior, unique animals, and barbecues when I think of ...

3 I imagine lots of tourists, terrible traffic, fantastic ice-cream, lots of ancient monuments, and the Vatican when I think of ...

4 I imagine thousands of busy people walking to work, tall skyscrapers, yellow taxis, really hot Julys, really cold Januarys, and the Statue of Liberty when I think of ...

2 Imagine a country or a city. Describe it to your class. Ask them to guess the place you are thinking of.

Vocabulary

Describing countries

1 Match the groups of adjectives in **A** with the nouns in **B**.

A	B
busy polluted noisy modern exciting	countryside
friendly helpful aggressive polite rude	weather
hilly mountainous flat wonderful unspoilt	food
awful dry changeable sunny wet	people
golden sandy beautiful crowded deserted	cities
spicy delicious tasty expensive lovely	beaches

2 Put the adjectives in the right column. Which ones don't have these stress patterns?

3 In pairs. Cover the left-hand part of the table.

1 How many adjectives can you remember?

2 Try saying them with the nouns – remember to use the correct stress pattern. *hilly countryside, mountainous countryside,* etc.

4 Which adjectives could describe your country?

Grammar
Comparatives and superlatives

1 How much do you know about the world? Circle the correct answers.

The most common first language in the world is **English / Chinese**, which is spoken by approximately **600 million / 1,200 million** people.

The largest country in the world is **Russia / Canada**, with a total area of over **17 million / 6 million** square kilometres. It is **70 / 7** times larger than the UK.

The biggest city in the world is **Tokyo / Mexico City**, with a population of about **30 million / 15 million**. The second biggest is **São Paulo / Calcutta**.

The highest mountain in the world is **Everest / K2**, which is **8,863 / 6,863** metres high. **Annapurna / K2**, the second highest, is **256 / 982** metres lower.

The most popular country with foreign visitors is **France / the USA**, with over **30 million / 60 million** a year.

The driest desert is the Atacama desert in **Chile / Mexico** – in some areas rain hasn't fallen for **400 / 4,000** years.

The sunniest place is Yuma, in **Peru / Arizona**, where there are over **4,000 / 10,000** hours of sunshine a year.

2 Compare your ideas with your partner.

3 How many comparative and superlative adjectives can you find?

Comparatives and superlatives

1 Complete the table. What are the rules for comparatives and superlatives? Are they the same in your language?

adjective	comparative	superlative
high	higher (than)	the highest
big	_____	_____
large	_____	_____
dry	_____	_____
sunny	_____	_____
common	_____	_____
popular	_____	_____

2 There are three irregular adjectives.

good	_____	_____
bad	_____	_____
far	_____	_____

3 We can also use *(not) as ... as* to compare things.
Geneva is as expensive as Tokyo.
The Amazon isn't as long as the Nile.

4 Look at this sentence. Where can you put these words? Which sentence is true?
much   a bit
England is bigger than Scotland.

Practice

 1 Listen to these dialogues. What is the pronunciation of *than* and *as*?

> **A** I think Japan is the safest country in the world.
> **B** Yes, but it's not as safe as Singapore.

> **A** I think English people are more polite than Americans.
> **B** Really? I think Americans are more polite than English people!

2 **In pairs.** Practise the dialogues. Try to sound exactly the same.

3 Make your own dialogues about these things.
1 New York / Paris / beautiful
2 Italian food / Spanish food / good
3 Australians / British people / friendly
4 Hong Kong / Singapore / modern
5 Scottish countryside / Irish countryside / unspoilt
6 India / China / interesting
7 Switzerland / Norway / expensive
8 Canada / the United States / big

4 Use four comparisons from exercise 3. For each one, make another sentence which means the same thing.
Paris is more beautiful than New York.
New York isn't as beautiful as Paris.

 5 **Against the clock** `3 minutes` Make as many sentences about these cities and countries as you can. Use a different adjective for each sentence.
Indian food is spicier than Spanish food.
Tokyo is more modern than Paris.

Rome	New York	Paris	New Zealand	Brazil
Spain	Argentina	Holland	India	China
Hong Kong	Sydney	Tokyo	Italy	Switzerland

Can you remember ...?
- ten adjectives to describe your country
- the three irregular comparatives and superlatives
- how to use *(not) as ... as*

Practice p.95

Speak out

Compare the following things in your country with the UK or another country that you know. Give as many examples as you can.

restaurants weather fashion shops
food traffic noise people buildings countryside

18
WHEN IN ROME

Speak for yourself

What's the most 'foreign' place you've been to? Why did it feel foreign to you? Think about these things.

- people
- language
- buildings
- weather
- customs
- music
- transport
- food

English in use

Politeness and customs

1 Read the text about customs. Match these headings to the paragraphs. Can you guess which country this advice is for?

Asking for things in a shop	Attracting attention	Topics of conversation
Attitudes to time	Talking to strangers	Offering and accepting
Saying hello	Introductions	

1 To say hello, say 'Good luck for the morning / afternoon / evening.' When you meet someone you know, shake hands and ask 'What's the news?' Men and women can shake hands but not kiss or hug in public. Good male friends can hug or hold hands.

2 When you are introduced to somebody, shake hands and say your name.

3 Say 'please' if you offer something to someone, for example 'Please have some tea.' Say 'Thank you' when you accept something.

4 Time isn't important here. The word for 'tomorrow' means 'sometime in the future' and the word for 'yesterday' means 'sometime in the past'. If you ask what time the bus or train will arrive, the usual answer is 'Rubber time', meaning 'Who knows?'

5 There is no word for 'please' when you ask for something. You can be more polite by saying 'Help' before you ask. Always use your right hand to give and receive.

6 To get someone's attention, say 'Excuse me.' To ask someone to repeat what they said, say 'What?'

7 It's OK to start conversations with strangers, to touch them, even to wake them up on a bus or train. Call a stranger 'father' or 'mother' if they are older than you, 'uncle' or 'sister' if they are the same age, or 'child'.

8 It's acceptable to ask people their name, address, telephone number, and questions like, 'Where are you going?', 'Where are you from?', 'Are you married?', and 'What is your religion?'

2 In pairs. Do you think these sentences about Britain are true (✓) or false (✗)? If they are false, change them so they are true.

1 Always shake hands with your friends when you meet them.
2 When you're introduced to someone you can just say 'Hello' and smile, or 'Pleased to meet you'.
3 British people don't say 'please' and 'thank you' much.
4 It doesn't matter if you're late for an appointment.
5 In shops you can just say 'Give me ...'
6 To get someone's attention, say 'Excuse me'.
7 British people love starting conversations with people they don't know – feel free to ask lots of personal questions.
8 You should be as polite as possible when talking to people you don't know.

Useful language

1 Here are some useful 'polite phrases'.

Would you like ... + infinitive / noun?
Could I have ... + noun?
Could you tell me ...?
Do you mind if I ... + verb?
You couldn't ... + verb, could you?
Excuse me, ... , please?

2 Complete the phrases in exercise 1 to make questions.

1 open the window
2 lend me 50p
3 a coffee, please
4 is this the way to the station
5 to see the photos I took
6 how much this costs

3 When / Where would you say these things? Who to?

Practice

1 Complete these questions. Match them with the responses.

1 Would you _____ a cup of coffee?
2 Hello, how _____ you?
3 _____ I have some aspirin, please?
4 _____ me, do you know the way to the stadium?
5 Have you _____ the time, please?
6 My _____ number's 0161 7663339.
7 Richard, can I _____ you to Nicola Rendall?
8 It's a lovely day, _____ it?

a Pleased to meet you, Nicola.
b I'm afraid I don't. I'm a stranger here myself. Sorry.
c Thanks, that'd be lovely.
d It's ten past ten.
e Yes, beautiful.
f Would you like 24 or 48?
g I'm fine, thanks. And you?
h Sorry, you couldn't repeat that, could you?

2 Listen and check your answers.

In English, *how* you say something is as important as *what* you say. To be polite you have to sound polite.

3 **In pairs.** Listen again and repeat the dialogues. Try to sound exactly the same.

4 Look at Tapescript 18.1 on *p.109*. Write down four key words from each dialogue. Then close your books and practise them.

 5 **Against the clock** `2 minutes` Look at the language in the **Useful language** box and make these sentences more polite.

  1 What's the time?

  2 Can I close the window?

  3 What did you say?

  4 Do you want a cup of coffee?

  5 Give me some aspirin.

  6 Where's the post office?

  7 Lend me some change for the phone.

  8 Be quiet.

6 Make dialogues from these cues.

	A	B
1	0131 7766121	repeat?
2	some stamps?	first or second class?
3	cup of tea?	thanks
4	introduce / Steven Richards	pleased
5	how / you?	not bad / you?
6	time?	8.20
7	way / New Theatre	sorry / stranger
8	horrible day	awful

Can you remember ...?

- three differences between customs in Indonesia and Britain
- four 'polite phrases'

Practice p.96

Speak out

1 **In groups.** Talk about politeness and customs in your country. Try to give examples. Think about these things.

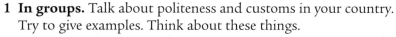

small talk

talking to strangers and older people

greetings and touching

misunderstandings

asking for things in a shop

time

introductions

offering, inviting, and accepting

2 What advice about customs would you give someone visiting your country from Britain?

19
LET'S CELEBRATE

In this lesson

- Saying dates
- Celebrations
- Words that go together

There are two ways of saying dates:
the twenty-fifth of December
December the twenty-fifth

Speak for yourself

1 These days are important in Britain. Do you know what they are?

25 December	1 January	14 February	24 December
31 October	5 November	31 December	

2 Which day(s) do you associate with these things?

fireworks	presents	children asking for sweets
cards	love	last-minute shopping
midnight	a day off work	

3 Think of four or five important dates for you / in your country. Why are they important?

10 September is important because it's my birthday.

5 August is important in my country because it's Independence Day.

Vocabulary

Special days

1 Think of two things that British people do on each of these days.

birthday   Christmas   New Year   Valentine's Day

2 Read the texts and match the days with the descriptions. Were your ideas right? Was there anything you didn't know?

1— In some countries they celebrate on the 24th, but in Britain we celebrate on the 25th. In our family we get up early and go to church. Then we come home and open the presents under the tree, which is always covered with beautiful decorations and lights. The bit I enjoy most is having a traditional dinner of turkey, roast potatoes, and vegetables, and because it's a special occasion we always …

2— Some people say the place to be is Princes Street in Edinburgh, where they have a huge street party. There's music, dancing, singing, and of course drinking, and at midnight everyone hugs and kisses everyone else, friends, family, and even complete strangers! Lots of people make resolutions which …

3— We had a postbox at school where you could put cards. Some people got lots of cards, and some people didn't get any. Most of the cards were handmade, with hearts and romantic poems on them. Now I send my girlfriend a single red rose and pretend I didn't. I proposed …

4—  Children love these. They get cards and presents from family and friends and they usually have a party with a cake and candles. We tell them to make a wish when they blow out the candles. The most important used to be your 21st but now it's your 18th. In some countries you buy the drinks, but in Britain …

Christmas
25/12
presents
tree

— birthday

SPECIAL DAYS

— Valentine's Day

New Year —

3 Match the endings of the final sentences with the texts.

... to her last year!   ... have a bottle of champagne.

... everyone else pays for you.   ... they can't usually keep!

4 In pairs. Make a word web for each of the celebrations, using words from the texts. Can you add any more things?

Practice

1 Mark the stressed syllable in these words.

celebrate	celebration	congratulate	congratulations
tradition	traditional	decorate	decoration
arrange	arrangement	champagne	occasion
resolution	romantic		

2 Where is the stress in words that end with *-tion* or *-sion*?

Words that go together   *Extra!*

a In pairs. Which verbs go with which nouns? (Some go with more than one.) Match them to the occasions on *p.50*.

give ——————— to your girlfriend

open   candles

go   a bottle of champagne

have   a cake

make   a wish

propose   dinner

cut   presents

blow out   resolutions

                to church

b **Against the clock** 3 minutes Use the words to make as many sentences about yourself as you can. Compare with a partner.

I gave my wife lots of presents for her birthday.

---

3 [○1] Listen. What would you say in each situation?

Many happy returns!	Merry Christmas!	Happy New Year!
Good luck!	Happy anniversary!	Congratulations!
Happy birthday!	Cheers!	

Can you remember ...?

• how to say dates

• three things people do on their birthday

• the stress in words that end with *-tion* or *-sion*

Practice p.98

Speak out

In groups. Describe a celebration in your country. Think about these things.

When is it?
    Is it for family and / or friends?

        What do people wear?

What preparations do they make?

        Do they play any special
        games or sing songs?

Do they give cards or presents?
    What kinds of presents do they give?

What food do they eat?
        How is it different to the UK?

Do you like it? Why / Why not?

Listen for yourself
Other countries

1 In groups. Look at these quotes from British people living abroad. Which countries could they be talking about?

1 Buses and trains are always on time - it's great!

2 I think the best thing is eating out. The food is delicious - hot, spicy, and cheap.

3 **The people are really hospitable. They're always inviting me into their houses, and introducing me to their families.**

4 Winter is depressing - we only get about five hours' daylight.

5 People say it's dangerous, but it never seems it to me.

2 ○1 You will hear an interview with Thérèse, a French woman, talking about her experience of living in Britain.

1 Listen to the questions. Write exactly what you hear.

1 What _____ thing _____ living _____ Britain?

2 _____ worst _____ ?

3 _____ miss _____ France?

4 _____ strangest _____ living in Britain?

5 _____ advice _____ give someone _____ Britain?

2 Compare with a partner.

3 Which answers do you think go with the questions above?

bring an umbrella	my family	the coffee	my friends
my boyfriend	the food	pubs and bars close early	

4 ○2 Listen to the interview and check.

5 ○3 Now listen to an interview with Jim, who lived in Ecuador.
1 How will the questions be different?
2 What answers does he give?

6 In pairs. Imagine you're living abroad. Interview one another, using the questions in exercise 2.

Jaffna

SRI LANKA

Colombo °Kandy △2,524m

Did you notice ...?

how many times Thérèse and Jim
repeat part of the question

Check in Tapescripts 20.2 and 20.3.
Why do they do it?

Practice *p.98*

Listen 2
What should I take?

1 | 04 | Jim's next job is in Sri Lanka. He's asking his friend Andrew for advice.

   1 Listen. Tick (✓) the topics they mention.

climate	places to visit
money	people
crime	food
things to do	restaurants
what to take	health
what to wear	nightlife

   2 Listen again and take notes.

   3 **In groups.** Compare your ideas.

2 What can you remember? Make sentences including these words.
He doesn't need to take many clothes.

clothes	shoes	a jumper	English books	glasses
safe	friendly	hot and spicy	water	

3 What advice would you give someone coming to live in your country?

Speak out

1 Write the names of these countries – don't write them in order.

a country

you'd like to live in
you'd like to visit but not live in
you wouldn't like to visit
where the food is bad
similar to your country
completely different from your country
with friendly people
with a good lifestyle

2 **In pairs.** Read your partner's list. Guess which category each country is in.

In this lesson

- Talking about magazines
- Obligation: *have to*, *don't have to*, and *mustn't*
- Pronunciation of *have*

Speak for yourself

1 Look at the magazine cover. What are the articles usually about in magazines like this?

2 Which of these articles do you think you would find?

The most exclusive shops in London

World financial crisis

YOUR HOROSCOPE FOR THIS WEEK

Banks raise interest rates again

101 ways to find love

Prime Minister to visit Far East

HOW TO BE HEALTHY

Perfect honeymoons

This year's fashion rules

Grammar

Obligation

1 Read extracts 1–6. Which articles are they from? Would they be in a women's magazine, a men's magazine, or both? How do you know?

1 ## For the best two weeks of your life

you have to go somewhere exotic. Forget Europe — you can go there any time. And you mustn't fly economy — this is the time to go first class …

2 If you can't afford the jackets, don't worry. You don't have to spend that much — just buy one of the beautiful ties. Then go upstairs for the best selection of luggage in London, and dream about travelling the world in style.

3 ## Virgo 24 August – 23 September

Career It's a difficult week for Virgos. You've got too much work to do, and too little time, and nobody understands your problems.

Money As usual, you never have enough money, but don't worry — you don't have to be rich to enjoy life!

Love You mustn't get involved in office romance — it's never a good idea, and you need all your time for work at the moment.

4

Short **hair. The shorter the better.**
Clothes have to work hard. Try to buy shirts and jackets that look good at work *and* after work.
The fashion experts say that black is this year's colour. Trousers, jumpers, shoes – everything has to be black. But we think the world needs colour.
Suits don't have to be boring – if you've got the money, buy Italian.

5

You don't have to wait for a man to ask you out. Surprise him, and make the first move yourself. Ask him for lunch, or a coffee after work …
Spend a weekend together in Paris – it's still the most romantic city in the world, and you can be there in three hours …
Remember – you don't have to be in a relationship. It's important to be independent sometimes …

6

You mustn't do too much exercise at first. It's important to choose a sport that you enjoy. Swimming is the best, but you have to go at least twice a week.

2 Are these sentences true (✓) or false (✗)? Which sentences in the extracts tell you?

1 It's good to go swimming three times a week. ☐
2 You need a lot of money to shop in London. ☐
3 Never fall in love with a colleague. ☐
4 It's important to have a boyfriend or girlfriend. ☐
5 Go to an exciting country on your honeymoon. ☐
6 Suits are boring. ☐
7 It's OK to get cheap flights for your honeymoon. ☐
8 You don't need lots of money to enjoy life. ☐
9 Do a lot of exercise immediately. ☐
10 Women can ask men out. ☐

3 In groups. Which ideas do you agree with?

Obligation

Use

Complete the sentences and match them to the uses.
I have to get up at 5.00 tomorrow, because…
She doesn't have to go to work tomorrow, because…
He mustn't wear jeans at work, because…

- no obligation
- prohibition
- obligation

Form

1 Complete the table for *have to*.

+ I / You / We / They _____ get up at 5.00 tomorrow.
   He / She _____

− I / You / We / They _____ wear a uniform.
   He / She _____

? What time _____ I / you / we / they _____ get up?
   What time _____ he / she _____ get up?

2 Correct the mistakes.

1 She's have to go now.
2 I am have to go home.
3 You mustn't to smoke.
4 I not have to take the exam.
5 Do I have got to come?
6 He's not have to wear a uniform.

Practice

1 Listen to these sentences from the horoscope. How is *have* pronounced?

You never have enough money.

You don't have to be rich.

2 Against the clock `3 minutes` Make as many sentences as you can.

Teachers		take exams.
Business people	(don't) have to	go to conferences.
Students		look smart at work.
I		work on Saturdays.
		travel a lot.
		get up early.

> *Have to* and *have got to* mean the same thing.
>
> *I have to go.*
>
> *I've got to go.*
>
> *Have got to* is more informal.

3 Can you add more sentences about yourself?

4 Complete these sentences with *have to*, *don't have to*, or *mustn't*. Which magazine article do they go with?

1 If you want to lose weight, you _____ eat less and exercise more.

2 Love is also hard to find, but you _____ be patient.

3 You _____ wear brown shoes with grey trousers.

4 You _____ do anything you don't want to – just be happy together.

5 You _____ phone him first – make him wait!

6 You _____ buy anything. Looking is half the fun.

5 Don't look at the texts. What can you remember?

1	suits / boring	6	wait for a man to ask you out
2	clothes / work hard	7	fly economy
3	do too much exercise at first	8	go swimming at least twice a week
4	go somewhere exotic	9	rich / enjoy life
5	everything / black	10	office romance

> **Can you remember ...?**
> • the difference between *mustn't* and *don't have to*
> • how to pronounce *have*
>
> **Practice p.98**

Speak out

1 In groups. What would you find in these magazine articles? Make sentences with *have to*, *don't have to*, and *mustn't*.

Top tips for a healthier you

What to wear to a wedding

How to be a model

How to make him / her love you

How to be successful at work

2 Compare your ideas – do you agree?

22
JUST LOOKING

Speak for yourself

1 **In pairs.** A memory test – when was the last time you bought these things?

a book	fast food
an item of clothing	a present for somebody
a CD	a train or plane ticket

2 Try to remember as much as you can about what happened. Think about these things.

- Where did you buy it?
- How much did it cost?
- How long did it take you to decide what to buy?

Vocabulary
Spending money

1 What shops or places would you do these things in?

- buy jeans
- buy painkillers
- have an eye test
- have a drink
- have dinner
- send a parcel
- have a haircut

- do the weekly shop
- buy a newspaper
- buy a ring
- see a film
- buy a film
- change money
- buy a novel

2 Which things can you do at these times in your country?

midnight   10.00 a.m.   7.00 p.m.   Sunday morning

English in use
Spending more money

 1 Here are ten requests connected with buying things.

  1 Listen and complete them.

    1 Excuse me, can you tell me _____ , please?

    2 Excuse me, do you think I could _____ ?

    3 I'd like to buy _____ .

    4 _____ *Casablanca*, please.

    5 Excuse me, could you tell me _____ the toothpaste, please?

    6 Can I have _____ , please?

    7 Could you tell me _____ ?

    8 Could you possibly _____ in one hour?

    9 Can I _____ you?

    10 Could I _____ for this afternoon, please?

  2 Compare your answers with your partner. Check in Tapescript 22.1 on *p.109.*

 2 Match each request with a response below. Listen and check.

  a Certainly. They'll be ready after lunch.

  b I think it's in aisle seven. I'll show you.

  c There you are. Screen two is on the left. Enjoy the film.

  d Standard 35 mm would be fine.

  e Certainly. Would you like 10, 20, or 50 units?

  f Sure. Can I have a look at it?

  g Yes, the fitting rooms are over there.

  h No, thanks. I'm just looking.

  i They're on the second floor.

  j Is that for a cut or a wash, cut, and blow dry?

3 Which dialogue would you hear in a clothes shop? Where would you hear the other dialogues?

Useful language

1 Look at these expressions in a clothes shop, and mark them **C** for customer and **A** for assistant.

Asking	Trying on	Paying
I'm just looking, thanks.	Could I try it / them on, please?	Can I pay by credit card?
Can I help you?	The fitting rooms are over there.	How would you like to pay?
What size would you like?	Any good?	Cash or credit card?
Have you got this in a size 12 / a medium?	It's a bit tight / big / small.	Your receipt's in the bag.
I'll just have a look.	Do you think I could try on a bigger one?	
I'll take it / them.		

2 Listen to this dialogue and tick (✓) the expressions you hear.

3 Which expressions could be useful for buying other things?

4 Compare these two questions. Which is more polite?

  Where are the CDs, please?   *Could you tell me where the CDs are, please?*

Practice

1 Against the clock `3 minutes` Make these sentences more polite.
1 I want to try it on.
2 Where's the shampoo?
3 Give me a phonecard.
4 I want to pay by credit card.
5 I want you to dry clean this suit today.
6 How much is this?
7 Give me a smaller one to try.
8 Where are the fitting rooms?

> Remember – it's important to *sound* polite.

2 `○ 4` Listen and check your ideas. Repeat the sentences and try to sound exactly the same.

3 In pairs. Make short dialogues which include these phrases.
A *Could I have a film for this camera, please?*
B *Would you like black and white or colour?*
A *Colour, please.*
1 black and white or colour?
2 where the travel books are?
3 dry clean this jacket?
4 battery for my camera?
5 shirt costs?
6 I'm sorry, we haven't got any fitting rooms.
7 wash, cut, and blow dry.
8 24 aspirin?
9 film starts?

> **Can you remember ...?**
> • six types of shop
> • six phrases you use or hear in a clothes shop
> **Practice p.99**

Speak out

1 In pairs. You are in a clothes shop. Decide what to say and have the conversation.

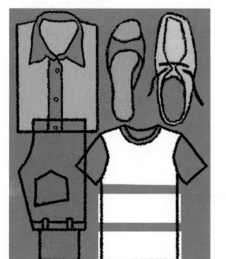

Shop assistant	Customer
Hello / help you?	try trousers on?
What size and colour / like?	small / medium / large / blue
fitting rooms / over there	Thank you
good?	bit big / smaller?
better?	Yes / how much
35.99	take them
how / pay?	cash / credit card
There you are / receipt / bag	Thank you
Thank you / bye	

2 Now change the details of the conversation (item of clothing, size, colour, price) and change roles.

3 Perform one of your dialogues for the class.

23 NOTHING TO WEAR

Speak for yourself

Find out if these statements are true (✓) or false (✗) by doing a class survey. If they are false, change them so that they are true.

1 No one wears earrings every day.
2 Not many of us buy second-hand clothes.
3 Only one of us has a tattoo.
4 All of us have changed our hairstyles recently.
5 We all usually wear make-up.
6 None of us has any designer clothes.
7 Nobody has more than ten pairs of shoes.
8 One of us never wears a watch.

Vocabulary

Clothes and accessories

1 Read the texts. What do they tell you about the three people?

> I usually wear a dark suit, a white shirt, and a tie to the office. I carry a briefcase with me, and if it's raining, an umbrella and raincoat. At home I wear a pair of old trousers, and a cardigan which smells of my pipe smoke.

> I have to wear a uniform. I hate the colours – brown and green. We have to wear skirts and a shirt and tie, and we can't wear make-up or jewellery. I can't wait for the weekend, and then I can wear what I want – jeans and a top, and lots of rings and bracelets. I love big earrings!

> To work I wear the same thing every day, white shirt, black tie, black jacket and trousers, and black shoes. And a hat when I'm on duty. We're not allowed to wear jewellery, it could be dangerous if we have to make an arrest, and no make-up either. At home, I usually wear something very casual, maybe joggers and a T-shirt, and trainers.

2 Read the texts again and underline all the clothes and accessories.

3 **In groups.** Complete the word web with as many clothes and accessories as possible.

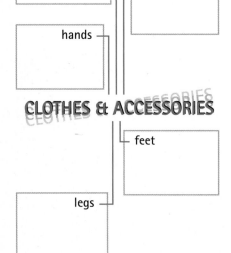

head — body

hands

CLOTHES & ACCESSORIES

feet

legs

Practice

1 Look at the word web again. Which things are only for men / women?

men	women

2 **Against the clock** `3 minutes` Make sentences about people in the class. Tick (✓) as many words in the word web as you can.

(Keiko) is wearing …
(David) has got …

3 Check the meaning of the verbs in italics.

Do you think this shirt *goes with* these trousers?
That hat really *suits* you.
This suit doesn't *fit* very well.
That jacket *looks* great.

4 **In groups.** Practise complimenting each other on your clothes.

I like your jumper – it really suits you / it looks great …

Can you remember …?

- three items of jewellery
- four informal items of clothing
- three things that only women wear

Practice p.100

Words that go together   *Extra!*

a **Match the words.**

three-piece	cotton	gold	leather	woollen	high-heeled
shirt	earrings	shoes	jumper	suit	watch strap

b **How many of the things have you got?**

Speak out

1 **In groups.** What would you wear in these situations?

- a wedding (not your own)
- a job interview
- a party
- to walk the dog

- at work
- after work
- on a first date
- at the weekend

2 Which of the situations would you need new clothes for?

24
MY GENERATION

In this lesson

- The last 40 years
- Listening: couples talking about old photographs
- Talking about important current events

Listen for yourself
When was that?

1 What do you know about the people and events in these pictures? Can you complete the years?

2 Check your ideas on *p.109*.

c 19 __ – __

b 1940 – __

d 1910 – __

f 1929 – __

a 19 __

e 19 __

g 19 __

 3 Listen to these people talking about the events above. Do they get the years right?

4 They often don't know the exact answer. Listen again and tick (✓) the phrases they use when they're not sure.

1 I'm not sure.
2 I don't know.
3 I think it was …
4 Something like that.
5 Could be.

6 I think so.
7 I may be wrong.
8 No idea.
9 I can't remember.
10 Perhaps.

5 What other famous people and events can you think of from the 1960s, 70s, 80s, and 90s?

Listen 2
The way we were

1 Look at these two photographs.

  1 When do you think they were taken?

  2 Describe the couples' clothes and hair.

2 Look at the beginning of the conversations. Match the photographs to the couples.

Susan	Look at this photo. I can't believe we looked like that!
Dave	I know, it's so embarrassing ...

Sam	Well, we haven't changed that much.
Daniel	Not really, no ...

3 Now listen to the two couples talking about the photographs.

  1 When were they taken?

  2 What people and things do they talk about?

clothes and jewellery	famous people	sport	music

Did you notice ...?

phrases which mean 1980–83, 1974–76, and 1967–69

Check in Tapescript 24.1.

`Practice p.100`

Speak out

1 What will people remember about this year in ten years' time? Think about these things.

2 **In groups.** Compare your ideas.

25
BEING A WORKER

In this lesson

- Present simple and continuous
- Adverbs of frequency
- Talking about lifestyles

Speak for yourself

Do you agree with these statements?

1 Housework isn't really work.
2 One parent should stay at home with the children.
3 Women are better than men at looking after children.
4 Parents should spend some time with their children every day.
5 Women can have children and a career.

Grammar
Present simple and continuous

1 Read the text. Which of the statements above would Mike and Tina agree with?

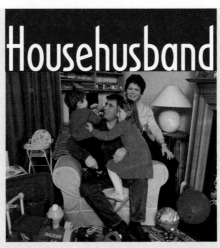

It's early evening and Mike Beaver, 41, is sitting in the living room of his suburban house near London. He's reading to his daughter Louise, six, and his baby son Eddie is playing with his toys. Aha, you think, Mike has come home from work and he's enjoying quality time with his children.

But you'd be wrong. Mike is a house-husband. He looks after the children full-time, and he does the same things any housewife does. He wakes the children up and gives them their breakfast, takes Louise to school, and one day a week takes Eddie to the nursery. Then he cleans the house, does the shopping, and picks the children up from school. He makes dinner for his wife Tina. Then he puts the children to bed – all while she's at work.

Tina is the director of a PR firm in London so she earns a good salary, but she works long hours. She goes to work at 7.00 in the morning and she often doesn't get home until 8 p.m., when the children are usually asleep, so she hardly ever sees them during the week. But at the weekend they spend time together. They go shopping, go for a family walk, the children sometimes invite friends over, and in the evening they all sit in front of the television. For these two days, Tina forgets her career, and she enjoys being with the children.

'Many people, especially men, don't believe me, but I'm enjoying life. I'm doing what I want to do,' says Mike. And what does Tina think? 'It means that I can have a career, which I love. And I admire Mike for being so good at what he does – he does a better job than I ever could!' she says with a smile.

2 **In groups.** Discuss these questions.
- What do you think of Mike's 'job'?
- Could you be like Mike? Would you marry someone like Mike? Why / Why not?

3 Look at the text again. Complete the gaps.

a He _____ to his daughter Louise.

b He _____ the children full-time.

4 What tenses are used in sentences **a** and **b**? Look at the text again and find three examples of each tense.

Present simple and continuous

Form

Complete the tables with the verb *work*.

Present simple		
+	**–**	**?**
I / You / We / They work.	_____ work.	_____ work?
He / She / It _____	_____	_____

Present continuous		
+	**–**	**?**
I'm working.	I'm _____ working.	_____ I working?
You / We / They _____	_____	
He / She / It _____	_____	

Use

1 Complete the rules with a, b, c, and d.

We use the present simple to talk about …
We use the present continuous to talk about …

a habits / regular events.   c what is happening now.

b temporary states.   d facts.

2 Do you have the same rules in your language?

3 Match the questions with the answers.

What do you do?	In a hotel until I can find a flat.
What are you doing?	In London.
Where do you live?	I work for a bank.
Where are you living?	Trying to find my wallet.

Adverbs of frequency

1 Find four adverbs of frequency in the text.

always ⇨ u_____ ⇨ o_____ ⇨ s_____ ⇨ h_____ e_____ ⇨ never

2 Do these words go before or after the verb? What about the verb *to be*? Check your ideas in the text.

Practice

1 What is the he / she / it form of these verbs?

1 Try saying them, and put them in the right column.

/s/	/z/	/ɪz/

sit	pass	look	understand
drive	go	speak	belong
start	work	kiss	put
make	earn	watch	do

2 Listen and check.

2 Here are some everyday activities.

1 Complete the gaps with a verb.

earn	get	make	take
work	go	sit	invite
clean	look	do	put

1 _____ after the children

2 _____ them to school

3 _____ home from work

4 _____ for a walk

5 _____ the shopping

6 _____ the children to bed

7 _____ friends over

8 _____ in front of the television

9 _____ long hours

10 _____ the house

11 _____ dinner

12 _____ a good salary

2 Who does these things – Mike, Tina, the children, or the whole family?

3 Compare yourself and your family with Mike and Tina – try to use adverbs of frequency.

Mike cleans the house, but I never do. My wife always does it.

 4 Listen to the dialogues. Match the people and the activities.

1 Jack and Chloe

2 David

3 Stephanie

4 Mike

5 John and Sara

6 Kate

5 In pairs. Ask and answer questions about the people.

'Is David doing the shopping?' 'No, he isn't, he's …'

'What are John and Sara doing?' 'They're …'

6 Listen again. What exactly do the people say? Check in Tapescript 25.2 on *p.110*. Repeat the dialogues and try to sound exactly the same.

Can you remember …?

• what Mike does every day

• five adverbs of frequency

• how to pronounce -s endings

Practice p.100

Speak out

1 You're going to interview someone about their lifestyle. Make as many questions as you can. Ask questions about these things, and try to use all the question words.

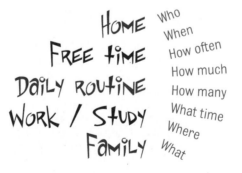

HOME

FREE time

Daily Routine

Work / Study

Family

Who
When
How often
How much
How many
What time
Where
What

2 In pairs. Ask and answer questions. Try to give as much information as you can.

3 How would you like your lifestyle to be different?

I usually get up at 7.00. I'd like to get up at 9.00!

26
ALL WORK AND NO PLAY

10–20 You find it easy to leave your work at work and relax at home … perhaps too easy! Make sure that you can work hard when it's important.

21–30 You work hard but you know when the time is right to relax and leave your work behind.

31–40 You are hopelessly addicted to work! Slow down, try to relax and enjoy life more. Are you working to live or living to work?

Speak for yourself

1 Try this questionnaire to see if you are addicted to work. Circle the numbers and add up your score.

ARE YOU a WORKaHOLiC?

1 = never   2 = rarely   3 = sometimes   4 = often

1	I find it difficult to find time to relax at home.	1 2 3 4
2	I take work home.	1 2 3 4
3	I spend my evenings and weekends working.	1 2 3 4
4	I spend my holidays worrying about work.	1 2 3 4
5	I work during coffee breaks and lunchtime.	1 2 3 4
6	I work late and go home late.	1 2 3 4
7	I forget about arrangements which are not work arrangements.	1 2 3 4
8	I talk about work when I'm socializing.	1 2 3 4
9	I find it difficult to find time to go out.	1 2 3 4
10	I like to be in control.	1 2 3 4

2 In groups. What kind of workers are you? Do you agree with the questionnaire?

Vocabulary
Work and study

1 Which of these words are connected with jobs, being a student, or both?

colleague	exams	library	business
revise	boss	deadline	study
office	learn	conference	meeting

2 In pairs. Use the words to talk about yourself.

I work in an office. I get on with my colleagues, but I hate my boss.

English in use
Giving advice

1 Look at this newspaper problem page. What's Susan's problem? What advice would you give her?

> My name's Susan. My husband runs his own business and I think he's a workaholic. He goes to work at 7.00 a.m., seven days a week, and doesn't come home until 8.00 or 9.00. He usually brings work home with him and when he doesn't, he spends the evening talking about it. We never go out any more. We don't even go on holiday together – last year I went away with friends. How can I make him understand that I want to spend more time with him?

2 Now read the advice. Which do you think is better? Why?

Auntie Ad

Men! They wine us, dine us, marry us, and then they forget about us. I think you should tell him that he has to look after you and his marriage, not his business. If I were you, I'd tell him to work less, and start spending more time with me! My advice is to arrange a surprise holiday for the two of you – and if he refuses to go, you should go without him!

Uncle Vice

Don't worry, Susan, this is perfectly normal. Your husband is married to his job and it seems as if he doesn't love you any more, but it's not true. Have you thought of talking to him about it? You should tell him how you feel, how much you miss him, and how much you want to go on holiday with him. Why don't you suggest a weekend in the country? Maybe this will make him think about his priorities in life.

3 What advice would you give Susan's husband?

Useful language

1 Read the problem page again. Complete these phrases.

You sh_____ / sh_____ + verb.

My _____ is to + verb.

If I _____ you, I'd + verb.

Have you _____ of + -ing form?

Why _____ you + verb?

2 Match the two parts of these sentences. What do you think the problems are?

1 I think	take some aspirin and go to bed.
2 My advice is to	take him to the vet?
3 If I were you,	you should get more exercise.
4 Have you thought of	I'd break the window.
5 Why don't you	having contact lenses?

3 🔲 Listen to the sentences.
1 Sentences 1, 2, and 3 – which words have the strongest stress?
2 Sentences 4 and 5 – which has rising intonation on the last syllable?

4 Listen again and repeat the sentences. Try to sound exactly the same.

Practice

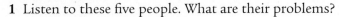

 1 Listen to these five people. What are their problems?

2 Match the problems with this advice.
- go but don't stay long
- stay until you find something more interesting
- go to see a doctor
- pay for the damage
- go by train

3 Practise giving the advice in different ways, using the **Useful language** box on *p.68*.

I think you should go by train.

My advice is to go by train.

 4 Listen and complete this dialogue for problem 1. How does the person ask for advice?

Jane	I've got a real _____ – I'm afraid _____ and my boss has asked me to fly to Paris _____ . What _____ you think _____ ?
Owen	_____ the meeting?
Jane	_____ at 10.00.
Owen	Well, _____ , I'd go by train _____ . Then _____ a bit of Paris, too.
Jane	_____ ! Thanks.

5 **In pairs.** Make short dialogues for the other four problems using this pattern.
- A Tell B that you have a problem, and ask for advice
- B Ask questions about the problem
- A Answer the questions, explain the problem
- B Offer advice
- A Accept the advice

> **Can you remember ...?**
> - one way of asking for advice
> - four ways of giving advice
>
> **Practice p.101**

Speak out

1 Think of a problem with work or study – it can be real or invented. Use the ideas below to help you.

exams
DEADLINES
money
travel
relationships

2 **In pairs.** Make a dialogue using the pattern in exercise 5.

3 Practise your dialogue and perform it for the class.

Speak for yourself

1 Match the beginnings and ends of these sayings.

1	All work and no play	a	make light work.
2	A woman's work	b	makes Jack a dull boy.
3	Work won't kill	c	is never done.
4	Many hands	d	but worry will.

2 Do you have similar sayings about work in your language? Translate them into English.

Vocabulary

Jobs and work

1 **Against the clock** 2 minutes Read the job adverts and answer the questions.

1 Which job pays most?
2 Which job doesn't pay at all?
3 Which needs most experience?
4 Which involves most travel?
5 Which isn't permanent?
6 Which job do you need a computer to apply for? Why?
7 Which jobs want people who've been to university?
8 Which could somebody leaving school apply for?

a

INTERNATIONAL VOLUNTARY WORK PROGRAMME

If you're planning to do voluntary work over the summer, take a look at what we have to offer. We send volunteers on four-week projects round the world, helping local communities.

Volunteers need no qualifications, should be aged 18+, enthusiastic, friendly, flexible, and enjoy working in a team.

For more information write to:

IVWP
19 Brook Street
Guildford
GU5 2JY

or visit our homepage at
www.ivwp.org

b *Can you see into the future?*

If you can, and you see yourself in IT, then we want to hear from you. We have vacancies for recent graduates in our Systems Support Network.

We offer:
– a starting salary in the region of £20K
– a full package of benefits including pension, health insurance, and flexitime
– challenging and varied work

You offer:
– a degree or diploma in computer science
– at least a year's experience in systems support
– enthusiasm, reliability, flexibility, and ambition

Interested? E-mail us.

networker@ssncv.co.uk

c **City of Eureka, California**

Parks and Beaches Manager

Full-time
Salary $4,500–$6,500 per month

Application closing date: Open until filled. Apply ASAP.

You will be responsible for the development and care of the city's parks and recreation facilities. You must have a degree in park management and four years' experience. The position requires excellent communication skills, and the ability to work independently. Applicants must have a California Driver's License.

For more information contact:
City of Eureka Personnel Department
10 Manchester Drive
Eureka California 90401

2 Look at the the vocabulary below. Match the headings with the groups of words. Add more words from the adverts.

- skills
- personality
- type of work
- pay
- benefits
- hours

highly-paid (not) well-paid low-paid	computer skills attention to detail driving languages	part-time overtime	boring interesting stressful	a company car long holidays	organized independent reliable patient

 3 Against the clock 3 minutes Make as many sentences as you can about your job (or a job you'd like to have), using the words in the chart.

Parts of speech   Extra!

a Look at the job adverts again. Complete these words.

Volunteers should be en _____ and fl _____ .

You offer en _____ and fl _____ .

b Use your dictionary to complete this table.

noun	adjective
reliability	_____
_____	patient
a friend	_____
a _____	challenging
ambition	_____
_____	responsible
_____	independent

c In groups. Use the words to describe yourself or the work you do.

Can you remember ...?

- two of the sayings about work
- three details about each job advert
- five adjectives to describe jobs

Practice p.102

Speak out

1 Which of these jobs would you be good at? Which would you like?

fitness instructor **nurse** **dentist** politician factory worker

2 Rank the jobs according to these things.

Pay Stress Skills needed Value to society

3 Compare your ideas.

In this lesson

- Talking about interview experiences
- Listening: two job interviews
- Having a job interview

Listen for yourself
Advice for interviewers

1 Have you ever had an interview? What can you remember about it?

- What was it for?
- Where was it?
- How did you feel?
- Who interviewed you?
- What did you wear?
- How long did it last?
- Did it go well?

2 Which of these topics do interviewers ask questions about?

- education
- politics
- personality
- hobbies
- salary
- religion
- health
- diet

3 Look at these ideas about how to be a good interviewer.

Advice for interviewers

1 Put a notice on the door so that people don't interrupt. Make sure the chairs are all the same height, and don't sit behind a desk.
2 Help the applicant to relax. Give them a cup of coffee and ask about their journey.
3 Don't make a decision in the first minute.
4 Don't be afraid to ask difficult questions – they often get the best answers.
5 Make a quick decision and tell the interviewees – nobody likes waiting to hear if they've got a job.

4 🔘1 Listen to a manager talking about the ideas. Complete the table.

1 How do you prepare the interview room?	
2 How do you help people relax at the start of the interview?	
3 Do you make snap decisions?	
4 What questions do people find difficult to answer?	
5 When do you tell people the result?	

5 Does he follow the advice for interviewers?

Listen 2

Two interviews

1 Complete these questions. Which does an interviewer ask and which does an interviewee ask?

1 Why / want / work for us?
2 Who / I work with?
3 How much / you earn / current job?
4 How much / I earn?
5 What / strengths / weaknesses?
6 Why / think / good at this job?
7 What / training opportunities?
8 Where / want to be / five years' time?
9 like / work / in a team?
10 possible / work flexitime?

2 ☐2 Listen and check. Which questions have Yes / No answers?

3 Listen again. Repeat the questions. Does the intonation rise (↗) or fall (↘) at the end?

4 ☐3 Look back at the IT job advert on *p.70*. Listen to two extracts from interviews for the job.

1 Which person gives better answers?
2 Which person would you give the job to? Why?

5 **In pairs.** What can you remember? Which person …

1 wants to live abroad? Where?
2 is making financial plans for the future? How do you know?
3 wants to stay in his new job for several years?
4 talks about qualifications?
5 works harder?
6 is more ambitious? How do you know?
7 is probably healthier? How do you know?
8 was late for the interview? Why?
9 wants to work flexitime? Why?
10 would earn more than before? How much more?

6 Listen again and check your ideas.

Did you notice …?

the word the interviewees used in these phrases
I'm _____ interested in…
I'd _____ like…
I _____ want to…

Check in Tapescript 28.3.

Practice *p.102*

Speak out

1 **In pairs.** You're going to have a job interview. Choose one of the jobs on *p.70*.

Interviewer

Think about these things:

- How will you help the interviewee to relax?
- What questions will you ask about education, experience, personal qualities, and future plans?
- Will you ask the interviewee if he / she has any questions?
- How will you finish the interview?

Interviewee

Think about these things:

- Why do you want the job?
- Why are you suitable for the job?
- What qualifications, skills, and personal qualities do you have?
- What questions will you ask about the job, the company, and the salary?

2 Have the interview.

29 HUMAN BEING

Speak for yourself

1 Match the ages on the left with the things on the right.

babies	go bald have children
children	leave home babysit settle down
teenagers	put on weight go on a cruise
twenty-somethings	eat sweets live on a pension
thirty-somethings	get married get their first job
middle-aged people	wear nappies go grey
retired people	play computer games get into trouble

2 Compare your ideas with a partner.

3 What are the most important events in a person's life? What have been the most important events in your life?

Vocabulary

Multi-word verbs

1 Look at these verbs from the texts. Use a dictionary and complete the sentences.

look after	grow up	give up
take up	settle down	look forward to

1 What do you want to be when you _____ ?

2 I'm really _____ seeing you again.

3 I'd like to _____ , get married, and have children.

4 I'm too young to _____ golf!

5 Who's going to _____ your cat while you're away?

6 I _____ smoking last year.

2 In pairs. Ask and answer these questions.

1 What did you want to be when you grew up?

2 Who looked after you when you were young?

3 Have you ever given anything up?

4 What are you looking forward to at the moment?

5 What sports or hobbies would you be interested in taking up?

6 What age do you think is best to settle down?

Grammar
The future

1 Read these texts and match them to the pictures. What life changes are the people talking about?

1 I was really tired of school, and I'm looking forward to university – I've finally grown up! I'm hoping to live in university accommodation for the first year, and after that I'd like to get a house with some friends. I'm going to study geography, but I want to have plenty of time for wild parties too.

2 I'm looking forward to earning more money, but I'm a bit worried about moving to Edinburgh. I'm going to stay with friends for a while, but I'd like to buy a place of my own soon, and I think Edinburgh's quite expensive ...

3 I'd like to take up painting, and I want to spend more time in the garden. After working for 40 years I'm not looking forward to having so much free time, but my grandchildren live just round the corner, so I'm planning to see a lot of them.

4 We're planning to have kids, maybe three or four, but not yet. Looking after them costs a fortune, and we'd like to have a few years on our own first – we're going to travel and see the world a bit. We're really looking forward to sharing our lives.

5 I'm looking forward to being single again, but it's difficult after you've been married. I feel as if it's time for a change – I hope to get a job outside London, and I'm going to give up smoking. At least we haven't got any children, so that isn't a problem.

2 Which people seem happiest about the future? Why?

3 How many different ways of talking about the future can you find in the texts? Check your ideas below.

The future

1 Look at these ways of talking about your future. Are they followed by a verb, an *-ing* form, or a noun?

I want to + _____

I'd like to + _____

I hope to / I'm hoping to + _____

I plan to / I'm planning to + _____

I'm looking forward to + _____ / _____

I'm going to + _____

2 How do we make negatives and questions with these forms?

3 Correct the mistakes in these sentences.

1 They're hoping get married soon.
2 He not want be doctor.
3 I'd really like taking up the piano.
4 I like to travel the world next year.
5 I'm looking forward to go to Brazil.
6 She wants be an engineer.
7 We're planning start a business.
8 I don't going to have any children.

Practice

I hope to ... and *I plan to ...* are more formal than *I'm hoping to ...* and *I'm planning to ...*

1 Look at these sentences. What can you say about each person? How old are they?

1 I'm going to go on a diet.
2 I'm looking forward to retiring.
3 I'm going to give up my job.
4 I'd like to hitchhike across the States.
5 I want to be a racing driver when I grow up.
6 I'm never going to get married again.
7 I'm hoping to study modern languages.
8 We're planning to sell the house when the children grow up and leave.

 2 Now listen to the sentences.

1 What happens to *to*?
2 What happens to *going to* and *want to*?

3 Repeat the sentences. Try to sound exactly the same.

4 ⏱ **Against the clock** 3 minutes Look at Angela and Janet. Make as many sentences about their futures as you can.

She's looking forward to going round the world.
She doesn't want to work in an office for ever.

5 Compare your sentences with the rest of the class. Can they tell you which person each sentence is about?

Speak out

1 **In pairs.** Make sentences about *your* future. Use the forms in this lesson.

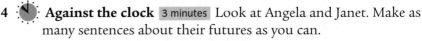

finish university have children (how many?)
have my own place   **get married** take exams
live abroad (where?)   be rich
go home   **have my own business**
travel the world   have a party
work (as a ...) retire do a parachute jump

Can you remember ...?
• five important life events
• three multi-word verbs
• how *to* is pronounced
Practice p.103

2 Compare your sentences with another pair. Do you have the same ideas about the future? Ask more questions.

A *I'd like to get married.*
B *Who to? When? Why?*

3 Have you got a 'life plan'?

30 GET WELL SOON

In this lesson

- Medical vocabulary
- Asking about and describing medical problems
- Talking about health when travelling

Speak for yourself

1 Read these texts. Which do you agree with?

Looking after yourself

For	Against
We should look after ourselves properly. We know it's dangerous to smoke, we know we shouldn't drink too much, and we know that diet is important. If we eat good food and take enough exercise we enjoy life more, and we enjoy it for longer. It's common sense.	It's ridiculous — people spend their lives worrying about what they eat and drink, going to the gym, and being unhappy about the way they live. And it doesn't make any difference. Eat what you want to eat, drink what you want to drink, and enjoy yourself. My granddad lived on fish and chips and Guinness, and he lived to 94.

2 What do you do to keep healthy? Think about these things.

- food
- alcohol
- cigarettes
- work
- exercise
- medical check-ups
- sleep

Vocabulary

Medical problems

1 In pairs. What do *you* do when you have these problems?

A I see a doctor.

B Oh, I carry on as normal.

a headache	a sore throat	a cold	a mosquito bite
flu	food poisoning	backache	a sprained ankle
sunburn	toothache	hiccups	a temperature
travel sickness	indigestion	stomach-ache	a cut finger

2 How many of the problems have you had in the last year?

There are six parts of the body that can go with *ache*. What are they?

English in use

What's the matter?

 1 Listen and complete the missing parts of the dialogue.

Helen	Hi, Nick. You _____ too good.
Nick	No, I feel _____.
Helen	_____?
Nick	I've got a _____ and my body _____ all over.
Helen	Oh dear. It sounds like flu to me. _____ go home?
Nick	_____ ...

2 Check in Tapescript 30.1 on *p.111*.

3 Practise the conversation.

Useful language

Look at these sentences. Connect the ones that mean the same thing.

1	I feel ill.	**a**	Are you all right?
2	What's the matter?	**b**	My stomach hurts.
3	You don't look too good.	**c**	Why don't you ... ?
4	Oh dear.	**d**	What's up?
5	Are you OK?	**e**	I feel awful.
6	I think you should ...	**f**	I'm sorry (to hear that).
7	I've got stomach-ache.	**g**	You don't look very well.

Practice

 1 Listen to these sentences. Which words are stressed? Repeat them and try to sound exactly the same.

You don't look very well.

Are you all right?

Oh dear.

I've got a splitting headache.

My back hurts.

I feel terrible.

I've got an awful cold.

 2 Now listen to these three dialogues. What's the problem, and what does the friend suggest?

	problem	friend suggests
1		
2		
3		

Practice p.104

What's the difference between *I'm cold* and *I've got a cold*?

Can you remember ...?
- eight medical problems
- three things to say to someone who looks ill

3 In pairs. Make a dialogue using these cues.

A	B
not look too good	No / terrible
What / matter?	awful toothache
dear / Why don't / dentist?	Yes / go tomorrow

4 Have similar conversations about these things.

a bad cold   a high temperature   terrible backache   indigestion

Speak out

1 In groups. Imagine you are travelling to a tropical country. What should you do to avoid getting ill? Complete the information below.

Before you go

Go to your doctor at least _____ weeks before you travel to find out what medication you need.

What to take

You should take a first aid kit containing:

_____   _____

_____   _____

_____   _____

_____   _____

While you are travelling

While you are on the plane, _____ .

If you suffer from travel sickness, _____ .

If you have jet lag when you arrive, _____ .

Avoid insect bites by _____ .

In hot climates drink lots of _____ .

Drink _____ water if possible.

Wash _____ before you eat it / them.

Don't eat _____ .

Keep out of the sun between _____

and _____ .

If you get sunburn, _____ .

If you are bitten by an animal, _____ .

2 What problems will you have if you don't do the things above?

3 What health advice would you give someone visiting your country?

31
MIND AND BODY

In this lesson
- Parts of the body, feelings, and emotions
- *-ed* and *-ing* adjectives
- Talking about similarities between animals and people

Speak for yourself

1 What animals do you associate with these things?

speed	wool	the sea	friendliness
stupidity	strength	organization	farms
cheese	malaria	racing	Christmas
feathers	honey	intelligence	Australia

2 If you were an animal, what would you like to be? Why?

Vocabulary
Bodies and minds

1 Read the first paragraph of the text. Who do you think is more intelligent? Why?

2 Read the rest of the text.

'Man has always thought that he is more intelligent than dolphins because he has achieved so much – the wheel, New York, wars, and so on – and all dolphins ever do is play around in the water having a good time. But dolphins have always believed that they are far more intelligent than humans – for exactly the same reasons.'

The Hitchhiker's Guide to the Galaxy, Douglas Adams

Humans and dolphins

have had a close relationship for thousands of years. There are lots of differences between people and dolphins, but in some ways the similarities are more interesting. Like humans, dolphins are highly intelligent animals. They have been trained to help underwater engineers, and there are also several examples of dolphins rescuing people who are drowning.

Dolphins

are social animals, often swimming in groups which can contain hundreds of individuals. They communicate with each other using a wide range of sounds. They also play, swimming, diving, and jumping out of the water together. They have a well-developed social structure. Female dolphins help each other during birth, while male dolphins often form a separate group. Young dolphins stay with their mothers for several years, and sometimes return to them in times of stress when they are adults. And dolphins help each other when they're in trouble, sometimes refusing to leave a wounded animal.

3 Close your book. How many similarities between humans and dolphins can you remember?

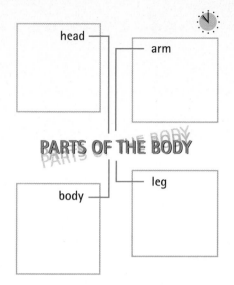

PARTS OF THE BODY

head — arm

body — leg

4 **Against the clock** [3 minutes] Complete the word web with as many parts of the body as possible.

5 Complete this table of feelings and emotions.

noun	adjective
anger	angry
	sad
	exciting / excited
boredom	/
	happy
	depressing / depressed
	disappointing / disappointed
surprise	/

6 Look at the adjectives. Which have four syllables? Where is the stress in the three-syllable ones?

> ### -ed and -ing adjectives *Extra!*
>
> Some adjectives can end in -ed or -ing, but the meaning is different.
> *Elephants are very **interesting** animals.* *I'm not **interested** in birds.*
> a What's the difference between *interesting* and *interested*?
> b Delete the incorrect words.
>   *The film I went to see was really bored / boring.*
>   *I was disappointed / disappointing when I failed the exam.*

7 Complete these sentences so they are true for you.

1 I feel very happy when I _____ .

2 It can be very disappointing when _____ .

3 I sometimes feel bored when _____ .

4 _____ can be very depressing.

5 I get angry if _____ .

8 **In groups.** Compare your ideas. Do you feel the same way?

Can you remember …?

• ten parts of the body

• four adjectives to describe emotions

• the difference between -ed and -ing adjectives

Practice p.105

Speak out

What similarities and differences can you think of between people and these animals?

ELEPHANTS

ants ants ants ants ants ants

CATS

chimpanzees

Think about these things.

• parts of the body

• emotions

• social structure

• behaviour

• language

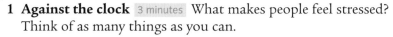

In this lesson

- Listening: stress management
- Discussing stress

Listen for yourself

What stresses you out?

1 **Against the clock** 3 minutes What makes people feel stressed? Think of as many things as you can.

2 Listen to these people answering the questions below. Complete the table.

	Sharon	Brad	Ben
What stresses you out?			
What do you do when you feel stressed?			

3 Complete these sentences.

1 I find _____ very relaxing.

2 _____ make(s) me nervous.

3 If I feel nervous, I _____ .

4 The night before a big day (an exam, for example), I _____ .

5 _____ give(s) me a headache.

6 I'm frightened of _____ .

7 I worry about _____ .

8 If I can't sleep I _____ .

9 I work best when _____ .

4 **In groups.** Compare your ideas. Try to explain them, and give each other advice.

Listen 2
Stress management

1 What do you think 'stress management' is?

2 Look at these ways of managing stress. Which do you think are good / bad ideas? Which have you used?

- Talk to yourself in a positive way.
- Take breaks during the day.
- Avoid coffee and alcohol.
- Go for a walk at lunchtime.
- Spend a day without your watch.
- Take exercise.
- Have fun.
- Say 'No'.
- Practise being happy.
- Eat more slowly.

 3 Listen to an expert talking about how to manage stress. Tick (✓) the ideas that she suggests.

4 **In pairs.** What can you remember? Complete these sentences.

1 Bad stress comes from situations when you feel _____ .

2 There are many symptoms of stress, such as _____ , _____ , or _____ .

3 Stress is like smoking – _____ .

4 You don't need tranquilisers, and _____ .

5 It's very important to _____ during the day.

6 You should eat healthy foods like _____ , _____ , and _____ .

5 Listen again and check.

Did you notice ...?
- a word which means *I can't believe it*
- a word which means *relaxing*

Check in Tapescript 32.1.

Practice p.105

Speak out

1 **In pairs.** Rank these things in order of stress.
1 = the most stressful and 10 = the least stressful.

- Public speaking
- Going out alone at night
- Going to the dentist
- Driving
- Flying
- Being in a crowd of people
- Friday the 13th
- Shopping
- Going on holiday
- Christmas

2 **In groups.** Compare your answers and give reasons.

3 Choose one of the things above. What advice would Janet Squire give to make it less stressful?

No stress   Some stress   More stress   too much stress

PRACTICE

01

Personal information

1 Match the words with the questions, and complete the questions.

1	First name(s)	a	What _____ you do?
2	Surname	b	Have you got any _____ ?
3	Sex	c	What's your _first_ name?
4	Age	d	Where are you _____ ?
5	Date of birth	e	Where _____ you live?
6	Place of birth	f	Where _____ you born?
7	Nationality	g	When were you _____ ?
8	Address	h	What's _____ surname?
9	Occupation	i	How _____ are you?
10	Marital status	j	What do you _____ in your spare time?
11	Dependants		
12	Interests	k	_____ you married?

2 Why are there only 11 questions in the right-hand column?

Question forms

3 Read the text about Sarah on *p.04*. Write the questions.

1 *Where does Sarah live?*
   In Eastbourne.
2 _____ do?
   She's an assistant hotel manager.
3 _____ ?
   A long-distance lorry driver.
4 _____ married?
   She was, but she isn't now.
5 _____ ?
   Three years ago.
6 _____ ?
   Yes, she has a daughter, Kate.
7 _____ Kate?
   She's five.
8 _____ ?
   From Wednesday to Saturday.
9 _____ Sarah's _____ ?
   She doesn't really have any.
10 _____ ?
   Near the town centre.

Jumbled dialogue

4 Read the text about George on *p.05*. Put the dialogue in the right order.

A Does he spend all his free time on his computer? ☐
A Is George married? 1
B I don't think so. George says it is not serious yet. He's too busy at work! ☐
B It's OK, but he's going to go back to university. ☐
A No, I don't. What a silly idea! ☐
B To study Internet design. He loves computers. ☐
A Why does he want to do that? ☐
B No, he's not, but he has a girlfriend, Robyn. ☐
A Does he have a good job? ☐
B No, he doesn't. I told you. He has a girlfriend and they go out two or three times a week. Why are you asking all these questions about George? Do you fancy him? ☐
A Oh! Are they in love with each other? ☐

Error correction

5 Correct the mistakes.

1	Live you in Barcelona?	Yes, I live.
	Do you live in Barcelona?	*Yes, I do.*
2	Is coming John too?	Yes, he comes.
3	What means this word?	I know not.
4	Where are you come from?	I from Barcelona.
5	How long you are staying here?	More three days.
6	Are you like learning English?	No, I no like. Is difficult.

Short answers

6 Think about your life. Write questions for these answers.

Question	Your answer
	Yes, I am.
	Yes, I do.
	No, I wasn't.
	Yes, I have.
	No, I didn't.
	Yes, I did.
	No, I can't.
	That's rather a personal question!

Filling in forms

1 Match the instructions with the items on the right. Which instruction has not been followed? Why?

1	Please use block capitals	a	<u>Mr</u> / Mrs / Ms / Miss / other
2	Please underline	b	always sometimes never ✓
3	Please circle	c	JOHN BROWN
4	For official use only	d	Yes ☒ No ☐
5	Tick as appropriate	e	Sex M Ⓕ
6	Indicate with a cross	f	Mon / Tues / ~~Wed~~ / ~~Thur~~ / ~~Fri~~
7	Delete as appropriate		

2 Complete this form.

VIXEN LOANS & CAPITAL

Please write in BLOCK CAPITALS and tick as appropriate.

Title _____

Surname _____

Full first names _____

Sex M ☐ F ☐

Date of birth _____

Place of birth _____

Nationality _____

Marital status single ☐ married ☐ divorced ☐ separated ☐

Number of dependent children _____

Address

House number _____

Street name _____

Town _____

Postcode (essential) _____

Telephone (inc. code) _____

Occupation _____

Present employer _____

Signature _____

Date _____

For official use only
OX 3 5 7 9 2 4 6 8 DMB

02

Vocabulary

1 Match the words.

1	stay	a book
2	go	a video
3	have	music
4	chat	in
5	get	on the phone
6	listen to	an early night
7	watch	out
8	read	a take-away

Social arrangements

2 Put the words in each line in the right order.

A evening you tomorrow are anything doing ?
Are you doing anything tomorrow evening ?

B special no nothing

A party you fancy do coming a to ?

B great sounds yes that
meeting a how drink about for first ?

A would nice be that

B Arms King's the ?

A like there I really don't it
go Black's to Café let's instead

B see OK there at you 8.00 ?

A you fine see

Refusing

3 Refuse these invitations and suggestions. Remember to give a reason.

1 Do you fancy going to the cinema tonight?
2 How about a trip to London this weekend?
3 Shall we go out for dinner tonight?
4 Would you like to go for a coffee?

03

Family vocabulary

1 Complete the sentences.

1 My father's brother is my ___*uncle*___ .
2 My mother's daughter is my _____ .
3 My sister's son is my _____ .
4 My father's father is my _____ .
5 My wife's mother-in-law is my _____ .
6 My son's daughter is my _____ .
7 My aunt's daughter is my _____ .
8 My father's sister is my _____ .

Describing people

2 Which is the odd one out?

1 long	short	curly	(tall)
2 young	40-ish	middle-aged	shy
3 lively	straight	outgoing	friendly
4 left-handed	fair-haired	broad-shouldered	green-eyed
5 black	ginger	elderly	blonde
6 beautiful	confident	attractive	gorgeous

04

Relationships

1 Complete the questions with these words.

> divorced   fancy   fallen in   married   out with
> love   split up   on with   argue

1 What is the longest you have ever been _out with_ anyone?
2 Would you ever get _____ from your husband or wife?
3 Do you get _____ your parents?
4 Do you believe in _____ ?
5 How many times have you _____ love?
6 Have you ever _____ with your boyfriend or girlfriend?
7 Who would you most like to get _____ to?
8 Who did you _____ when you were younger?
9 Who do you _____ most with?

2 Match the questions above with these answers.

a ☐ My teacher, Mrs Haddock. Unfortunately she was married and fifteen years older than me.
b ☐ Only if there was no alternative. First, I would try to save the relationship.
c ☐ More times than I can remember.
d ☐ Yes, but only when I don't see them.
e ☐ Yes. When I was younger, I wasn't very good at staying with one person for long.
f ☐ My sister, but we're always good friends afterwards.
g ☐ I'm already married!
h ☐ 1 About three years, and then we got married.
i ☐ Yes, 100%.

Useful expressions

3 Read tapescript 4.2 on *p.106*. Complete these sentences.

1 _____ we get on OK.
2 I want him to be tall, _____ , and _____ .
3 It wasn't exactly love _____ !
4 I was _____ when we decided to get married.

05

Past simple

1 Complete the text.

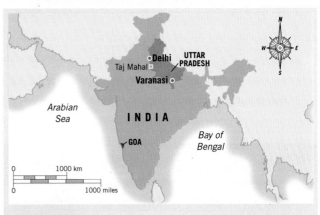

Last year I ¹w _ent_ _____ to India for a holiday with my girlfriend. We ²f _____ with British Airways to Delhi. We ³s _____ there for about three weeks. For the first two weeks we ⁴t _____ round Uttar Pradesh. We ⁵d _____ a lot of sightseeing, and we ⁶s _____ the Taj Mahal and Varanasi. For the last week we ⁷w _____ to Goa, where we ⁸s _____ most of the time on the beach. It ⁹w _____ a marvellous experience. The people ¹⁰w _____ very friendly, and the food ¹¹w _____ delicious. We ¹²a _____ all kinds of different curries and ¹³d _____ the local beer, Kingfisher. The holiday only ¹⁴c _____ about $1,000 dollars each, so it ¹⁵w _____ very cheap. We ¹⁶w _____ to stay for another three weeks.

Past simple and continuous

2 Complete the sentences.

1 When I _woke up_ (wake up) four elephants _were circling_ (circle) the camp.
2 It _____ (be) a beautiful morning – the sun _____ (rise) over the Andes, and the air _____ (be) clear and cold.
3 I _____ (drink) retsina, _____ (look) at the Mediterranean, and _____ (think) about dinner when the message _____ (arrive).
4 The ice _____ (melt) – we _____ (have to) move fast.
5 One minute the monkeys _____ (scream) in the tree-tops – the next minute, silence.
6 I _____ (arrive) at 8.00 a.m. Two hours later, hundreds of people _____ (walk) along the wall.

3 Match the sentences above to these countries.

> the Antarctic   China   Tanzania
> Greece   Chile   Brazil

Error correction

4 Correct the mistakes.

1 I decided I wanted to travelled around Vietnam.
   I decided I wanted to travel around Vietnam.

2 Something strange did happen to me yesterday.

3 I couldn't ring you last night because I not have your phone number.

4 When I was younger, my parents taked me on holiday every year.

5 I skied in the Alps when I felt over and breaked my leg.

6 I stayed in a cheap hotel when someone was stealing my passport.

7 I forgotted to buy it.

8 I was go on a business trip last week.

9 Where are my keys? I'm sure I putted them on the table.

10 I saw a lot of wildlife when I was drive across Africa.

Pronunciation

5 How many syllables do these past tenses have?

stopped	1	walked	☐
watched	☐	started	☐
waited	☐	married	☐
decided	☐	answered	☐
visited	☐	arranged	☐
changed	☐	asked	☐

-ed endings

6 Put the verbs in the correct column.

/ɪd/	/d/	/t/
		stopped

06

Transport vocabulary

1 What are these forms of transport?

1	rac	_car_	6	botomiker _____
2	itax	_____	7	napel _____
3	chaco	_____	8	narti _____
4	yerrf	_____	9	bute _____
5	cleblicy	_____	10	sub _____

2 Match the verbs and the nouns (some verbs go with more than one noun).

1	get on	a car
2	get off	a bus
3	get into	a plane
4	get out of	a taxi
5	ride	a bicycle
6	fly	a motorbike
7	drive	a train
8	take	a horse

Travel word web

3 Complete the word web with these words.

check in   terminal   ticket inspector   station
get off   check-in   pilot   ticket office   platform
take off   airport   departure lounge   driver
get on   flight attendant   arrive   land

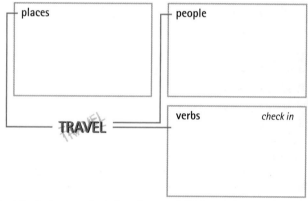

4 Mark the words **A** for air travel, **T** for train travel, **B** for both.

Travel signs

5 Where would you see these signs – a plane, train, or bus?

1 **Do not lean out of the window**   *train*

2 Do not flush while at station

3 **Exact fare please**

4 Do not speak to the driver whilst in motion

5 In case of emergency, pull chain

6 Stand clear of the doors

7 Fasten your seatbelt

8 Emergency Exit

9 Engaged

Train travel and hotels

6 Mark these lines **T** for train travel and **H** for hotel booking.

☐ *T* Can you tell me when the next Manchester train is?

☐ *H* I'd like to make a reservation, please.

☐ When for?

☐ Standard, please.

☐ For 22 January.

☐ Certainly. Could I have your name and phone number?

☐ It's at 9.22.

☐ That's £36.80, please.

☐ Can I have a return?

☐ A double with bathroom, please.

☐ First or standard?

☐ And what kind of room would you like?

7 Put the lines in order to make two conversations.

07

Travel advice

1 Match the travel advice to these places.

Ireland   Moscow   the Caribbean

1 People wear light cotton clothes all year round. The style is always casual. You should wear a tie (though not necessarily a jacket) for business.

2 It can be very hot and humid in summer, and extremely cold in winter – it's important to take the right clothes, though you can easily buy extra clothes there if necessary.

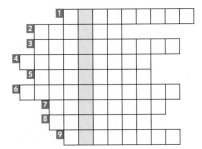

3 A raincoat or an umbrella is a necessity – it's one of the wettest parts of Europe. The climate is generally mild, but it can get chilly in the evenings even during the summer, especially if you're walking in the country.

4 There are many beautiful beaches, but the water can be cold! If you're determined to swim, the warmest water is in the south-east.

5 If you're going to travel between islands by boat, take some plastic bags to put your things in – especially your camera and documents.

6 A phrasebook is useful – very few people speak any English if you need directions, for example. Also, try to learn the alphabet before you go, or you may have trouble understanding signs and notices.

Travel vocabulary

2 Complete the puzzle to find a country.

1 You need these to power your personal stereo or torch.

2 You wear these instead of trousers in hot weather.

3 These protect your eyes from the sun.

4 This might be useful to find your way around.

5 You might wear this if it rains.

6 You need this for dry skin.

7 This is very useful to carry everything in when you travel.

8 You might wear these on your feet on the beach.

9 These are useful if your hotel is noisy!

Compound nouns

3 Match the two parts.

1 alarm	cream
2 traveller's	towel
3 money	clock
4 walking	bag
5 sun	screw
6 beach	licence
7 cork	cheques
8 driving	boots
9 cassette	belt
10 sleeping	recorder

4 Write sentences with the words in exercise 3.
You need an alarm clock if you have an early flight.

Multi-word verbs

5 Complete the sentences.

1 When did you __*get*__ back from your holiday?

2 It's very hot, I think I'll _____ on my sun hat.

3 I can't _____ up my mind whether to go to Nepal or Mexico for my holiday.

4 It was late, so I _____ into my sleeping bag and went to sleep.

5 I'm really _____ forward to going away.

6 I hope my parents will be at the airport to _____ me up when I arrive.

7 They _____ off at about 6 o'clock in the morning, and they reached the top three hours later.

Holiday incidents

1 These pictures tell a story. Can you put them in the right order?

2 Complete the story and check your ideas.

Last February I ¹ _went_ to Brazil on a lecture tour. At the end of the tour my wife ² f____ to Rio to join me ³ f____ a holiday. We ⁴ h____ a wonderful time. On the last day we went ⁵ f____ one more walk on the seafront. The sun was ⁶ s____, and people ⁷ w____ swimming and playing ⁸ f____, and we sat and watched. We were ⁹ w____ back to the hotel when I suddenly realized I'd left my jacket on the seat. All my money and the plane tickets ¹⁰ w____ in the hotel, but my passport ¹¹ w____ in one of the pockets. I went ¹² b____ but it wasn't there. In a complete panic we ran to the hotel – our flight was leaving in three ¹³ h____. We ¹⁴ w____ running across the lobby when the ¹⁵ r____ called to us, and she ¹⁶ h____ my jacket and passport. 'Where did you get that?' I ¹⁷ a____. 'One of the hotel porters was ¹⁸ p____ football on the beach, and he ¹⁹ s____ you leave your jacket, so he ²⁰ p____ it up and brought it here', she replied. A miracle.

3 Write a new story with this information.
Last April I went to ...
April / New York / holiday
fantastic time
last day / top of Empire State Building
restaurant / incredible view
walk back / hotel / realize / bag / restaurant
passport / hotel key / money / bag
go back / not there
ran / hotel / receptionist / shout / bag!
'Where / get?'
'Waiter / find / key / bring / here.'

4 Read tapescript 8.4 on *p.107*. Complete these sentences.

1 Wasn't it 'the _____ of a _____'?

2 It was _____ fantastic.

3 The kids had a _____ time.

4 Yes, it was really bad _____.

Writing postcards

1 Read the postcard and answer these questions.
1 Where's Groves?
2 How much longer is he staying?
3 Is he enjoying himself?

2 Tick (✓) the things he mentions.
people   food   weather   things he's done
things he's going to do   countryside   accommodation

3 Find adjectives which mean:
1 very beautiful
2 very good (x3)
3 very cold

4 Imagine you are in a hot, sunny country on holiday. Write a postcard to a friend. Mention five of the things in exercise 2.

Day, not date — Friday

Dear + first name — Dear Jill,
Put a comma after the name

Hello from Canada!

In postcards we can leave out articles and the verb *to be* — Having a wonderful time! Weather freezing – having to wear all my clothes whenever I go outside! I'm staying in a fantastic hotel in Kenora, a small town by the lakes. The scenery's gorgeous. Pubs and restaurants are great! Tomorrow I'm flying to Churchill to see some polar bears!

See you in a couple of weeks.

Best wishes, All the best, Love, (family and close friends) — Love,

Groves xx

Dr Jill Coates
6 Ashford Road
Whitstable
Kent
CT5 7JX
United Kingdom

Past participles

1 Complete the crossword.

across		down	
1 steal	14 see	2 take	11 throw
4 work	15 fell	3 have	13 travel
5 drive	16 fly	4 write	17 leave
8 come	19 be	6 begin	18 wear
10 get	21 live	7 go	20 make
12 eat	22 ride	9 rise	

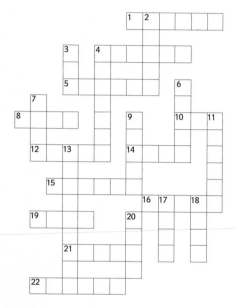

Have you ever ...?

2 Complete these questions with verbs from the crossword. Answer with short answers, and give more information where you can.

1 Have you ever *written* a poem?
Yes, I have. I wrote one when I was at school.
2 Have you ever _____ a sports car?
3 Have you ever _____ in a helicopter?
4 Have you ever _____ a camel?
5 Have you ever _____ to Scotland?
6 Have you ever _____ snails?
7 Have you ever _____ in love at first sight?
8 Have you ever _____ a cake?
9 Have you ever _____ an eclipse?
10 Have you ever _____ a jumper in bed?

Error correction

3 Correct the mistakes.

1 There's been an e-mail for you last night.
There was an e-mail for you last night.
2 Marlowe hasn't written *Twelfth Night*, Shakespeare has.
3 We knew him since he was a boy.
4 I have drunk a lot of wine last night.
5 She has been ill a week ago.
6 I have been born earlier than 1960.
7 What a fantastic photo. Have you taken it yourself?
8 How have you broken your leg?
9 It's the second time I was here in sunny Hastings.
10 The first time I have seen her I have fallen in love.

Present perfect and past simple

4 Make sentences with the past simple or the present perfect.

1 I / meet / my new boss / yesterday
I met my new boss yesterday.
2 I / eat / too much chocolate / today
3 You / ever / eat / frogs' legs ?
4 I / start / new job / last week
5 I / go on holiday / three weeks ago
6 I / not go swimming / this year
7 She / phone me / two minutes ago
8 He / have / mobile phone / since last year

5 Write appropriate answers to these questions.

1 Have you been away this year?
2 Have you ever written an e-mail in English?
3 What did you have for breakfast this morning?
4 What did you do yesterday evening?
5 How many times have you been to the cinema this year?
6 When did you last go to the cinema?
7 Did you go away last year?

been and *gone*

6 Choose the correct word.

1 Where have you (been) / gone? I was here half an hour ago.
2 Where has Peter **been** / **gone**? He's not at his desk.
3 Have you **been** / **gone** anywhere interesting recently?
4 I've **been** / **gone** to the bank. Back soon.
5 Have you ever **been** / **gone** to Buenos Aires?

10

Useful language

1 Complete the sentences.

1 I'm sorry, I *don't understand* .
2 Could you r _____ t _____ , please?
3 I'm sorry, I d _____ q _____ catch t _____ .
4 Could y _____ s _____ a bit more s _____ , p _____ ?
5 I'm sorry, I c _____ quite h _____ you.
6 Y _____ couldn't s _____ that again, c _____ you?
7 C _____ y _____ s _____ up a bit, p _____ ?
8 H _____ d _____ y _____ spell t _____ ?

Using a phone

2 Number the instructions in the right order.

- ☐ Insert more coins when the display flashes.
- ☐ Listen for the dialling tone.
- ☐ When you hear the dialling tone, insert coins.
- ☐ 1 Pick up the receiver.
- ☐ When the person you are calling answers, press the 'ANSWER' button.
- ☐ Dial the number you require.
- ☐ To end the call, replace the receiver.
- ☐ Listen for the ringing tone.
- ☐ If you hear the engaged tone, hang up.

Telephone vocabulary

3 Complete the sentences with these words.

> cut off   wrong number   hold on   hang up
> extension   ring   engaged / busy   ring back
> area code   bad line

1 Why don't you give me a _ring_ when you get home?
2 My _____ is 01424 and my number is 778823.
3 This is a very _____ . Can you hear me OK?
4 Sorry, I think you've got the _____ . This is the library not the sports centre.
5 Hello again. Did you _____ or were we _____ ?
6 I'm sorry, her line is _____ at the moment. Would you like to _____ later?
7 Can I speak to Jason Lombard on _____ 245, please?
8 _____ , I'll just get him.

Formal / informal phoning

4 Correct the mistakes in this formal phone call.

A Good morning, Okapi Software. How are you?
   Good morning, Okapi Software. How may I help you?
B I want to talk to Mr Singh.
A Who are you?
B I'm Dr Max Crisp.
A Wait a minute, Dr Max.
B OK.
A Mr Singh is engaged. Will you hang up?
B No, thanks, I ring him up later.
A Would you like a message?
B Could you say him I called?
A Sorry, no, I can't.
B OK, see you later.
A It was nice talking to you.

11

Technology vocabulary

1 Match the verbs and the nouns (some verbs go with more than one noun).

1 log on
2 plug in
3 send
4 answer
5 hang up
6 turn up
7 turn off
8 open
9 receive
10 pick up

> a TV
> an e-mail
> a computer
> a letter
> a telephone
> a radio

look, see, watch

2 Choose the correct verb.

1 Don't turn it off! I'm (watching) / looking at / seeing this programme!
2 Hey, come over here and **watch** / **look at** this picture.
3 I'd like to **see** / **watch** / **look at** you soon.
4 **Listen to** / **Hear** me when I'm **talking** / **saying** to you!
5 Shh. What's that? I can **hear** / **listen to** a noise.
6 A The film was brilliant!
   B I missed it. **Tell** / **Say** / **Speak** me what happened.
7 A I **spoke** / **told** / **said** to Sue this morning.
   B What did she **speak** / **talk** / **say** / **tell**?

Writing messages

1 Rewrite these messages as complete sentences.

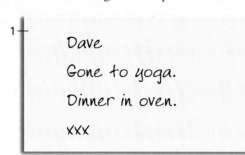

1.
> Dave
> Gone to yoga.
> Dinner in oven.
> xxx

Dave, I've gone to my yoga class. Your dinner's in the oven. Lots of love.

2.
> Peter
> Sorry, can't meet at 7.00.
> Outside cinema at 8.00, OK?
> Sue

3.
> Julia
> Gone to dentist. Back by 3.00.
> If Sue phones, take message.
> Vicky

4.
> Bill, computers crashed!
> Contacted IT dept. Coming at 11.30.

5.
> Bruce
> WHERE ARE YOU????
> Cancelled 2 appts this a.m. M.D. rang.
> Problems! Geraldine

2 Write short messages. Cross out the words you don't need.

1. Phil, Becky rang ~~you~~ last night. ~~She said she~~ wants to talk ~~to you~~ about ~~your~~ holiday plans.

2. Bill, the TV has been repaired. The only thing wrong with the TV was the plug! It cost £65!! Sue

3. Ben, Benita phoned you last night. She wants you to call her back. She says it's very urgent.

4. Paul, I've borrowed £20 from your wallet. I'll pay you back this evening. I'll see you in the restaurant at 8.00, Paula

5. Angela, I'm really sorry, but I can't meet you at the weekend. I've got too much work to do. Maybe we could meet the weekend after?

12

Short responses

1 Match the sentences with the responses.

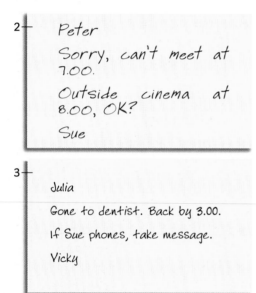

1. He's been to Rio. —— Neither did I.
2. He's never late for a date. So was I.
3. They didn't see it. So have I.
4. He's buying a computer next week. So am I.
5. I spent the whole weekend surfing. So did I.
6. They were bitten by mosquitoes. Neither am I.
7. He doesn't think men and women are different. Neither do I.

Useful expressions

2 Read tapescript 12.2 on *p.108*. Complete these sentences.

1. Can you _____ us some examples?
2. Men _____ to use more imperatives.
3. I've never _____ that.
4. It _____ a lot _____ the individual.

13

Money verbs

1 Complete the sentences.

1. I'd love to go on holiday, but I can't <u>afford</u> to this year.
2. How much do you _____ on shoes each year?
3. Can you _____ me some money? I'll pay you back later.
4. I want to buy a new car, so I'm going to _____ a little each month until I've got enough.
5. How will you _____ for it? Cash or credit card?
6. What a lovely new dress! How much did it _____ ?

Money vocabulary

2 Match the opposites.

1. buy   cheap
2. win   borrow
3. expensive sell
4. spend   lose
5. lend   save

First conditional

3 Write complete sentences.

1 If / sunny / we / go / beach
   If it's sunny, we'll go to the beach.
2 If I / pass / my exams / go / university
3 If you / eat too much / feel sick
4 She / get sunburn / if / stay out in the sun
5 If I / earn enough this year / go on holiday
6 I / save money / if / walk to work
7 I / not worry about money / if / win the lottery
8 If you / not ask me / I / not do it
9 If I / work hard / be able to afford a car
10 I / miss the game / if / stay at home

Present simple or *will*?

4 Complete the slogans, and match them to these products.

> a pen   a CD player   a diamond ring
> moisturiser   instant coffee   a PC

1 If you like music you *'ll love* (love) this.
2 When you taste it you _____ (not believe) how good it is.
3 You'll notice the change in your skin as soon as you _____ (use) it.
4 You'll feel the difference before you _____ (start) writing.
5 If you want to show you love her, this _____ (last) forever.
6 We'll give you free advice and on-site servicing for a year after you _____ (buy) it.

if, when, before, after, as soon as

5 Choose the best word to complete the sentences.

1 I'll meet you **after** / (**before**) the film starts.
2 She'll ring you **if** / **when** she gets to the airport.
3 I'll do it **before** / **when** I've got time.
4 They'll drive to Edinburgh **if** / **as soon as** they can't get a flight.
5 We really want a new car. We'll buy one **after** / **as soon as** we get paid.
6 We'll cancel the game **if** / **when** it rains.

14

Restaurant vocabulary

1 Complete the puzzle to find a typical British meal.

1 Something you usually eat with a burger.
2 You put rubbish in here.
3 The first meal of the day.
4 It's red and you eat it with 1.
5 You carry food and drinks on this.
6 A list of food and drinks in a restaurant.
7 The evening meal.
8 Knives, forks, and spoons.
9 Something to put over the table to keep it clean.
10 Red or white?
11 Mineral water with bubbles.
12 Something you can drink out of.

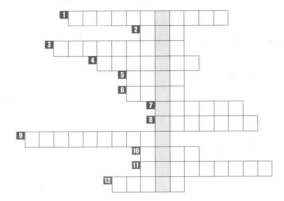

Restaurant dialogue

2 Put in more words to make this dialogue more realistic.

Waiter	Ready?	*Are you ready to order?*
Customer	Soup.	
Waiter	White bread?	
Customer	Brown.	
Waiter	Follow?	
Customer	Trout.	
Waiter	Rice?	
Customer	Potatoes.	
Waiter	Drink?	
Customer	Beer.	
Waiter	No beer. Wine?	
Customer	Red.	
Waiter	Thanks.	

15

Containers

1 What are these containers?

1 anc   *can*   4 xob   _____

2 teltob   _____   5 tancor   _____

3 tapeck _____   6 nti   _____

2 What are these things? Match them with the containers above.

a ☐ act odof   _____

b ☐ sprsic   _____

c ☐ newi   _____

d ☐ suetiss   _____

e ☐ eCko   _____

f ☐ faperurgit eciju _____

Supermarket word web

3 Complete the word web. Put four things in each part.

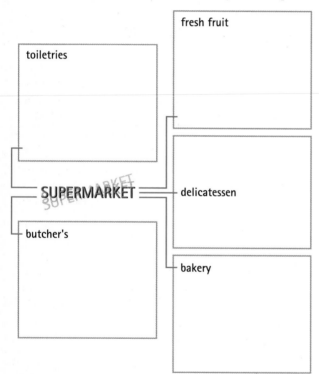

Countable / uncountable nouns

4 Put the words in the word web in the right column.

Countable	Uncountable

5 Tick (✓) the correct sentences.

1 How much money have you got? ✓
How many money have you got?

2 Did the teacher give us much homework?
Did the teacher give us many homework?
Did the teacher give us any homework?

3 I haven't seen many films.
I haven't seen much films.
I haven't seen any films.

4 I've just made any tea.
I've just made some tea.
I've just made a few tea.

5 There were a few people in the restaurant.
There were a little people in the restaurant.

6 I haven't taken any photographs.
I haven't taken many photographs.
I haven't taken no photographs.

16

Likes and dislikes

1 Write the numbers on the line.

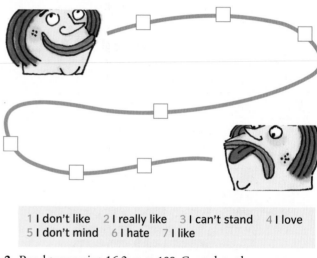

1 I don't like   2 I really like   3 I can't stand   4 I love
5 I don't mind   6 I hate   7 I like

2 Read tapescript 16.2 on *p.108*. Complete these sentences.

1 I _____ driving during the day.

2 I _____ doing the shopping whatever time it is, I _____ all the people.

3 The kids _____ it.

4 We _____ when we shop.

3 Put the words in the right order.

1 clothes I buying hate
I hate buying clothes.

2 really shopaholics shopping love

3 hate I the shopping Christmas doing

4 don't supermarket week I once mind to going the a

5 window Saturday I shopping on really love afternoons

6 can't mind I stand shopping but don't shoppers I the

7 really you think families do enjoy together shopping ?

17

Comparatives and superlatives

1 Read the text about restaurants in the States and Britain. Complete the gaps with comparative and superlative adjectives.

> **AMERICAN RESTAURANTS** offer a lot more choice than British restaurants, and the food is ¹ _more unusual_ (unusual), which I think is ² _____ (good). In Britain the choice is tea or coffee, but in America there are maybe 20 different types of coffee. For breakfast, you can have rye toast, sultana toast, wholewheat toast, eggs scrambled, over easy, sunny side up. But ordering takes much ³ _____ (long)! In Britain ordering is much ⁴ _____ (simple) and ⁵ _____ (quick).
>
> The service in America is probably the ⁶ _____ (good) and ⁷ _____ (fast) in the world but you have to leave ⁸ _____ (large) tips than in Britain. American waitresses' wages are ⁹ _____ (low), so waitresses are usually much ¹⁰ _____ (friendly) in America!
>
> It's ¹¹ _____ (difficult) to be a vegetarian in Britain, or have a special diet. But in America you can have whatever you want, and the restaurants are open ¹² _____ (late).
>
> Portions are much ¹³ _____ (large), much ¹⁴ _____ (generous) than here, and it's ¹⁵ _____ (cheap). Perhaps that's why some Americans are among the ¹⁶ _____ (fat) people in the world, so maybe more is not always ¹⁷ _____ (good).

2 Five students came to Britain in successive years. They each stayed for different lengths of time. When did they arrive and how long did they stay?

1 Paula came to Britain in 1994. She was here two years longer than José.
2 Alicia came to Britain two years before Paula and stayed twice as long as José.
3 In 1995 Mohammed came to Britain for five years (a year longer than Mako).
4 José was the first of the five to come to Britain, and he stayed for a year.

	year	number of years
Paula	1994	
Alicia		
José		
Mako		
Mohammed		

Error correction

3 Correct the mistakes.

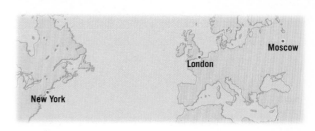

1 Which is more far from London – New York or Moscow?
Which is further from London – New York or Moscow?
2 Switzerland is the more mountainous country in Europe.
3 Melbourne isn't as big than Sydney.
4 Thai food is the more tasty I've ever eaten.
5 My French is even more bad than my Spanish.
6 The Atacama Desert is more dry than the Sahara.

Describing countries

4 Match the first impressions to the places.

> Singapore   Paris   Canada   Brazil   Italy

1 It sometimes feels like England but it's a lot bigger, wider, and flatter. It's much colder in the winter – minus 50 or 60. Good beer. Much better than the States.

2 It's much warmer than Britain, and a lot more crowded, there are lots of people around. They're friendlier and more enthusiastic. There's a lot less alcohol drunk than I imagined, they do everything on Coca-Cola.

3 The food and wine are fantastic. The people are so much nicer and friendlier than where I come from. We go out at night and eat and eat. Restaurants stay open really late.

4 It's more stylish than London, more beautiful. The architecture is fascinating, there's always something to look at. It isn't as friendly, but outside the city everything's a lot slower.

5 The streets are so clean, it must be the cleanest and safest place in the world, and maybe one of the busiest ... very cosmopolitan.

Writing informal letters

1 Read this letter.

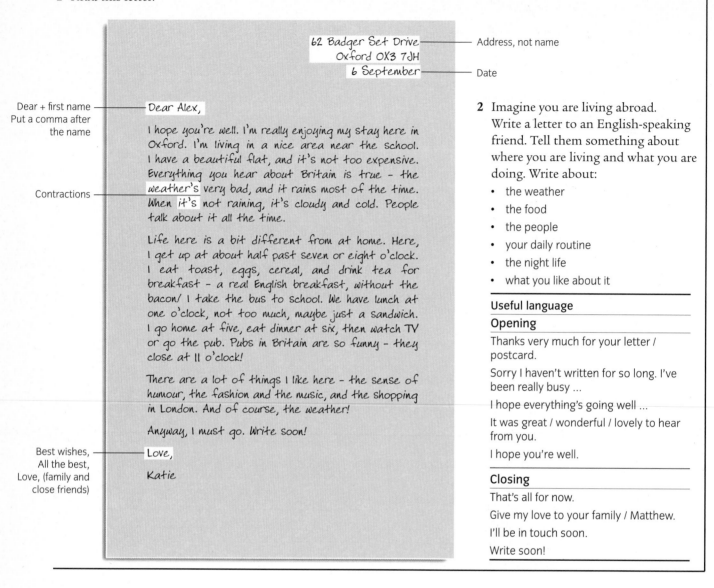

62 Badger Set Drive — Address, not name
Oxford OX3 7JH
6 September — Date

Dear + first name
Put a comma after
the name

Dear Alex,

I hope you're well. I'm really enjoying my stay here in Oxford. I'm living in a nice area near the school. I have a beautiful flat, and it's not too expensive. Everything you hear about Britain is true - the weather's very bad, and it rains most of the time. When it's not raining, it's cloudy and cold. People talk about it all the time.

Contractions

Life here is a bit different from at home. Here, I get up at about half past seven or eight o'clock. I eat toast, eggs, cereal, and drink tea for breakfast - a real English breakfast, without the bacon! I take the bus to school. We have lunch at one o'clock, not too much, maybe just a sandwich. I go home at five, eat dinner at six, then watch TV or go the pub. Pubs in Britain are so funny - they close at 11 o'clock!

There are a lot of things I like here - the sense of humour, the fashion and the music, and the shopping in London. And of course, the weather!

Anyway, I must go. Write soon!

Best wishes,
All the best,
Love, (family and close friends)

Love,

Katie

2 Imagine you are living abroad. Write a letter to an English-speaking friend. Tell them something about where you are living and what you are doing. Write about:

- the weather
- the food
- the people
- your daily routine
- the night life
- what you like about it

Useful language

Opening

Thanks very much for your letter / postcard.

Sorry I haven't written for so long. I've been really busy ...

I hope everything's going well ...

It was great / wonderful / lovely to hear from you.

I hope you're well.

Closing

That's all for now.

Give my love to your family / Matthew.

I'll be in touch soon.

Write soon!

18

Polite language

1 Put these words in the right order to make questions.

1 you would biscuit like a ?
Would you like a biscuit?

2 newspaper at have a could the I look ?

3 please tell the me you time could ?

4 if here you do I sit mind ?

5 lend could couldn't you you me £10.00 ?

6 the this the office way to post is ?

7 you how are hi ?

8 I friend to you can my Harvey introduce ?

9 a it beautiful it's isn't day ?

10 you for to like would day out the go ?

2 Match the questions in exercise 1 with these answers.

a ☐ No, not at all, go ahead.

b ☐ What a lovely idea.

c ☐ Not too bad, you?

d ☐ Sorry, I've only got £5.00 myself.

e ☐ 1 ☐ Chocolate Hobnobs! My favourite!

e ☐ Pleased to meet you.

f ☐ Isn't it?

g ☐ It's about twelve, I think.

h ☐ Yes, carry straight on, you can't miss it.

j ☐ Do you want the main bit or the sports section?

Politeness and customs

3 Choose the correct answer(s) for Britain.

1 You say this when you want to get past somebody:
- ☐ Excuse me.
- ☐ I'm coming through.
- ☐ Pardon.

2 You say this when you want to attract someone's attention:
- ☐ Listen!
- ☐ Excuse me.
- ☐ Please.

3 You can say this to a stranger:
- ☐ Lovely day, isn't it?
- ☐ Are you married?
- ☐ How much do you earn?

4 Which is better?
- ☐ Please can I borrow your pen?
- ☐ Can I borrow your pen, please?
- ☐ Give me your pen, please.

5 When someone says 'How do you do?' you say:
- ☐ Fine, thanks.
- ☐ I'm a student.
- ☐ Pleased to meet you.

6 If you have an appointment for 11.00, you should arrive at:
- ☐ 10.55.
- ☐ 11.10.
- ☐ 11.30.

7 You can shake hands with people:
- ☐ when you first meet them.
- ☐ every time you see them.
- ☐ when you meet them again after a long time.

Writing cards

Match the occasions and the messages.

1 Your friend's birthday.
2 Someone you know is getting married.
3 Your friend is taking an important exam tomorrow.
4 Someone you know is celebrating 50 years of marriage.
5 Your friend has just passed an important English exam.
6 Someone is ill.
7 A friend has just had a baby.
8 Someone is leaving work aged 65.
9 You are invited to a New Year's party.
10 A friend has failed her driving test.

a Congratulations and best wishes for the future!
b Congratulations! I knew you could do it.
c Many happy returns. Have a wonderful day!
d Thank you for asking me. I'd love to come.
e Happy anniversary!
f Congratulations! I hope you're all doing well.
g Get well soon.
h Better luck next time.
i Best wishes for your retirement.
j Good luck! I'll keep my fingers crossed.

Useful language

Thank you (very much) for + noun / -ing
  Thank you very much for a lovely weekend / for taking me to the airport.
Congratulations on + noun / -ing
  Congratulations on your exam results / on passing your driving test.
Best wishes for + noun
  Best wishes for the future / for your birthday.
Good luck with + noun
  Good luck with your new job / with your exams.
I hope + verb
  I hope you feel better soon / you have a wonderful day.

19

Prepositions

1 Complete the sentences with *in*, *on*, *at*, or nothing.

1 We always have roast turkey _on_ Christmas Day.
2 It's my birthday _____ next month.
3 I was born _____ 7 o'clock _____ the morning.
4 We usually have a national holiday _____ the spring.
5 I'm getting married _____ tomorrow morning.
6 Where I come from, people often give each other money _____ New Year.
7 What were the New Year's celebrations like _____ 31 December 1999?
8 I had my 21st birthday _____ 1996.
9 I'll see you _____ the weekend.
10 Most people try to get married _____ May or June.

Celebration vocabulary

2 Which is the odd one out?

1 **Christmas**
a presents b tree c decorations (d) a wish

2 **birthday**
a cards b a party c fireworks d flowers

3 **Valentine's Day**
a roses b hearts c a street party d champagne

4 **New Year**
a dancing b 21st c resolutions d hugs and kisses

20

Nationalities

1 Complete the crossword.

across	down
1 the Netherlands	2 Thailand
3 Brazil	4 Italy
6 Japan	5 France
11 Hungary	7 the USA
13 Ireland	8 Spain
14 Kenya	9 Poland
	10 Turkey
	12 Greece

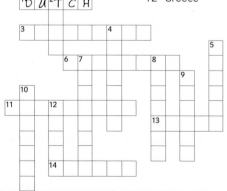

Useful expressions

2 Read tapescript 20.4 on p.109. Complete these sentences.

1 I wanted to ask you _____ .
2 Not much, _____ anything.
3 When I came back, I had _____ of stuff.
4 _____ else you can think of?

21

(don't) have to

1 Are these sentences true (✓) or false (✗) for your country?

1 You have to drive on the right.
2 People have to carry an identity card or passport.
3 Young men have to join the army.
4 You don't have to vote.
5 You have to pay 10% tax in restaurants.
6 You don't have to tip taxi drivers.
7 You have to pay to go to university.
8 Most schoolchildren have to wear uniforms.
9 You have to have a licence for your TV.
10 You don't have to wear a crash helmet on a motorbike.

(don't) have to / mustn't

2 Complete the sentences.

1 You _don't have to_ wear a tie for the occasion, but you can if you want to.
2 You _____ be mad to work here – but it helps!
3 If you want to pay over the phone you _____ use a credit card.
4 If you want to get fit, you _____ exercise more and eat less. You _____ eat too much fried food.
5 You _____ have money to have style. Style can be very economical.
6 You _____ think that the important thing is *what* people wear. The important thing is *how* they wear it.
7 If you want to be a successful manager, you _____ dress like a junior secretary.
8 You _____ wear very expensive clothes, but remember that what you wear affects your success with the opposite sex.

22

Signs and notices

1 Match the signs and notices with the places.

> a cinema a shop a cashpoint a restaurant a park
> a nightclub a supermarket checkout a car park

1 **Clean it up!**

2 **NO JEANS**

3 Shoplifters will be prosecuted

4 *Twelve items or fewer*

5 PATRONS PLEASE NOTE
THIS IS A NO SMOKING
A U D I T O R I U M

6 **Pay and display**

7 Insert card here **with stripe
facing down and to the right**

8 Credit cards not accepted

Shopping word web

2 Complete the word web. Put three things in each part.

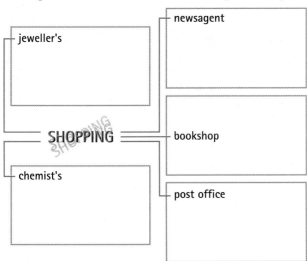

jeweller's

newsagent

SHOPPING

bookshop

chemist's

post office

3 Match the sentences and the objects.

1 Would you like 10, 20, or 50 units?
2 I need a size nine, in black.
3 I am a 16 neck. Should I get the medium or large?
4 I'd like a standard 35mm, 36 exposures, please.
5 Gold or platinum?
6 I think a size 10 is the same as a 42.
7 The hood is detachable.
8 It's got a great pair of speakers.

a shirt
a ring
a phonecard
a rainjacket
a stereo
a dress
shoes
a film

Taking something back

4 Put the words in each line in the right order.

A afternoon good can you I help how ?
Good afternoon, how can I help you?
B please refund this I'd a on sweater like
not enough big really it's
A your receipt you have do ?
B you are here yes
A you do have credit card your ?
your it account to refund we need
B it is certainly here
A here you could sign ?
much thank you goodbye very

UK consumer quiz

5 Choose the correct answer.

> 1 **If you buy a waterproof jacket and it leaks, what is the shop obliged to do?**
>   a Send it back to the manufacturer for repair.
>   b Exchange it for another one.
>   c Give you your money back.
>
> 2 **If you break something in a shop and there is a notice that says 'All breakages must be paid for', do you have to pay?**
>   a No. Not if it was a genuine accident.
>   b Yes. If there is a notice you have to pay.
>   c Yes. Even if there is no notice displayed you have to pay.
>
>
>
> 3 **If you buy wine in a French supermarket, how much are you allowed to bring into the UK?**
>   a Ninety litres.
>   b Twenty litres.
>   c Two litres.
>
> 4 **If you buy a CD and you don't like it, can you take it back?**
>   a Yes, the shop has to give you your money back if you want.
>   b It depends on the shop – some will change it and some won't.
>   c No. Once you buy it, it's yours.
>
> 5 **If a flight is delayed for three hours, what is the airline obliged to do?**
>   a Nothing.
>   b Give you vouchers for food and drink.
>   c Give you compensation.

23

Clothes and accessories

1 Match the numbers and the items.

☐ earrings	☐ lipstick
☐ watch	☐ shirt
☐ skirt	☐ zip
☐ pocket	☐ button
☐ collar	☐ sleeve
☐ belt	☐ jacket
☐ handbag	☐ glasses
☐ high-heeled shoes	☐ hat
☐ necklace	☐ umbrella
☐ tie	☐ jeans

2 Match the descriptions and the items.

> earrings   make-up   pipe   jumper
> suit   hard hat   socks   shoes

1 They're my most comfortable pair, the leather's really soft.

2 I hardly ever smoke it, but I find it very relaxing.

3 They're my favourites, gold with a sun design.

4 I don't like wearing it, but it's an important safety precaution.

5 My grandmother made it for me last Christmas. I wear it once a year!

6 It's the city uniform, everyone wears one.

7 **I prefer not to wear it, or maybe just a bit of lipstick.**

8 They always disappear in the washing machine!

24

When was that?

1 Match the events and the years.

1 Bob Marley died. — 1962

2 Nelson Mandela became president of South Africa. — 1981

3 France won the World Cup. — 1998

4 Yuri Gagarin was the first man to fly in space. — 1978

5 Margaret Thatcher resigned as Prime Minister. — 1974

6 Prince Charles married Lady Diana Spencer. — 1961

7 There were three Popes in one year. — 1994

8 The film *Titanic* was the biggest blockbuster ever made. — 1981

9 Sean Connery starred as James Bond in the first Bond film, *Dr No*. — 1998

10 Abba had their first number 1 hit in the UK charts, *Waterloo*. — 1990

Useful expressions

2 Read tapescript 24.2 on *p.110*. Complete these sentences.

1 I really can't _____ it.

2 I was _____ what to do with my life.

3 I've _____ got that hat.

4 I think this was _____ Diana died.

25

Present simple

1 Look at the table and make sentences about Mike, Tina, and yourself.

		Mike	Tina	you
1	get up / 7.00 a.m.	usually	often	?
2	work / office	never	always	?
3	have a beer / before dinner	always	sometimes	?
4	eat out / restaurant	occasionally	often	?

1 *Mike usually gets up at 7.00 a.m.*
  Tina often _____
  I _____

2 Mike _____
  Tina _____
  I _____

3 Mike _____
  Tina _____
  I _____

4 Mike _____
  Tina _____
  I _____

Present simple and continuous

2 Correct the mistakes.

1 This car is belonging to my father.
This car belongs to my father.
2 She is speaks English.
3 He go shopping twice a week.
4 The film starts now.
5 After I am eating breakfast, I get dressed.
6 She lives not in London.
7 Where you work?
8 She is not understanding the problem.
9 A Do you like chocolate?
B Yes, I like.
10 Why you no get a job?

3 Choose the correct verb form.

1 A **Do you eat** / Are you eating meat?
B No, I'm a vegetarian, but **I eat** / **I'm eating** fish.
2 A How **do you do** / **are you doing**?
B Pleased to meet you.
3 A How **do you do** / **are you doing**?
B Not very well, this exercise is difficult.
4 A Where **do you live** / **are you living**?
B In a bed and breakfast at the moment.
5 A What **do you have** / **are you having** for breakfast?
B Usually just coffee.
6 A What **do you want** / **are you wanting** for breakfast?
B Nothing, I'm in a hurry.
7 A What **do you do** / **are you doing**?
B I'm an engineer.
8 A What **do you do** / **are you doing**?
B Not much, just watching TV.
9 A **Does it rain** / **Is it raining**?
B Yes, take an umbrella.
10 A **Does it snow** / **Is it snowing** much here?
B Only in winter.

Pronunciation

4 Look back at the text about Mike and Tina on *p.64*. Find the verbs ending in *-s*, and put them in the correct column.

/s/	/z/

26

Work and study vocabulary

1 Complete the words to find the name of a job.

1 You take lots of these at university.
2 A big meeting, often once a year.
3 Where a businessperson works.
4 Someone who can't stop working.
5 A place where you can borrow books.
6 Someone at university.
7 To look back at your work before an exam.
8 Someone who works with you.
9 If you apply for a job you may have one of these.

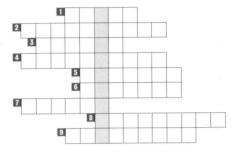

Giving advice

2 Read the text. Write six sentences giving advice to a friend who is going for a job interview tomorrow.
If I were you, I'd wear a suit.

We asked ten managers why people do badly in interviews.
Is it because they don't wear the right clothes, or they're
too confident (or not confident enough)?
Here are their top six answers:

1 Poor personal appearance
2 Nervousness and lack of self-confidence
3 Give vague answers to questions
4 Arrive late for the interview
5 Fail to ask questions about the job
6 Too interested in money and salary

3 Put the dialogue in the right order.

☐ Yes, that's right. They're already talking about downsizing and making people redundant. I could lose my job.

☐ Maybe I will. Thanks for the advice.

☐ Hello, Rodney. I hear Global are taking over your company.

☐ No, not yet. No one in Global is talking to me, and that's a bad sign.

☐ Are you sure? Have you talked to the new Managing Director?

☐ Well, if I were you I wouldn't wait to be asked. I'd ring the Managing Director and ask to see him.

27

Jobs and work

1 How many work-related words can you find? There are fifteen.

```
G  P  (S  E  C  R  E  T  A  R  Y) R  V  S
M  R  K  O  V  E  R  T  I  M  E  D  B  H
A  O  D  A  T  V  O  L  U  N  T  E  E  R
N  F  C  M  J  X  G  D  A  Q  T  U  R  E
A  E  H  D  E  M  U  S  I  C  I  A  N  N
G  S  U  E  X  E  P  D  T  U  P  R  G  G
E  S  P  N  S  C  I  E  N  T  I  S  T  L
R  I  A  T  U  H  S  Y  U  H  P  Q  E  A
R  O  L  I  R  A  C  O  D  R  S  C  A  W
S  N  W  S  G  N  S  A  L  A  R  Y  C  Y
J  A  V  T  E  I  H  Z  A  Y  O  F  H  E
L  L  Y  W  O  C  E  N  G  I  N  E  E  R
J  O  U  R  N  A  L  I  S  T  J  H  R  T
```

2 Match the words with these definitions.

1 A person who types letters and answers the phone.
secretary

2 A person whose job is to repair machines.

3 Someone who studies science.

4 A doctor who performs operations.

5 A person who looks after people's teeth.

6 Someone whose job is to give advice on legal matters.

7 A person whose job is to collect, write, or publish news.

8 A person who designs or builds roads, bridges, etc.

9 Someone who works for no pay.

10 Someone who helps students learn.

11 A person whose job is to play a musical instrument.

12 Any person whose job needs advanced training.

13 Someone with a senior position in a company.

14 The money you earn.

15 Extra hours that you work.

3 Complete the sentences.

1 I only work ___*part-time*___ , usually 15 hours a week.

2 My job isn't w _____ - _____ but it's very i _____ .

3 She's lucky, she's got a c _____ car.

4 I won't get the job, I haven't got the right q _____ .

5 I need a holiday, my work is much too s _____ .

6 He's r _____ for the whole project.

Word stress

4 Complete the table by marking the number of syllables and stressed syllables.

professional	oOoo	profession	oOo
musician		music	
technician		technology	
surgeon		surgery	
dentist		dentistry	
volunteer		voluntary	
journalist		journalism	
engineer		engineering	
architect		architecture	
secretary		secretarial	

28

Applying for a job

1 Complete the text.

> offer   fill in   application   successful   education   advertisement   company   letter   career   invite

> First you see an 1 *advertisement* for a job. You send off for an 2 _____ form. You 3 _____ the form and send it off with a covering 4 _____ and your CV. If they like your application, they 5 _____ you for an interview. They ask you questions about your 6 _____ and 7 _____ history, and you ask them questions about the job and the 8 _____ . If your interview is 9 _____ , they 10 _____ you the job.

Useful expressions

2 Read tapescript 28.3 on *p.110*. Complete these sentences.

1 I _____ have to work on Saturdays and Sundays.

2 I'd like more money too, _____ !

3 It took me _____ to get here.

4 I'm _____ I'm late.

Writing formal letters

1 Read this letter of application.

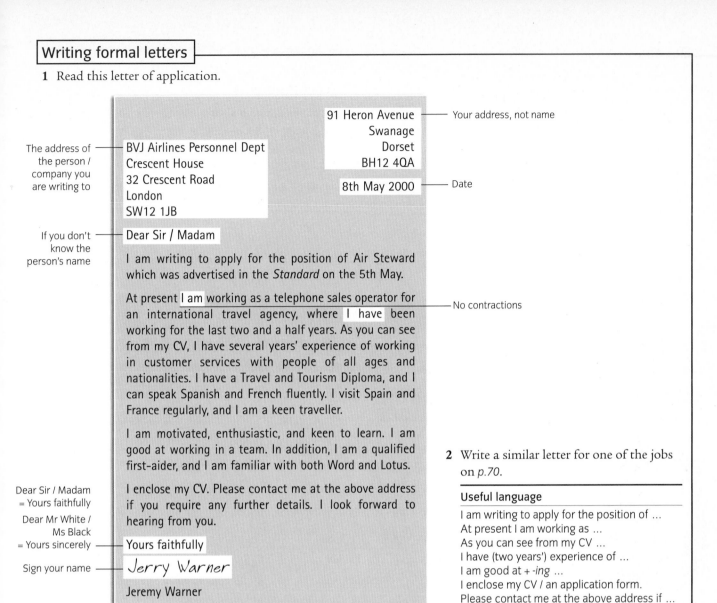

The address of the person / company you are writing to

BVJ Airlines Personnel Dept
Crescent House
32 Crescent Road
London
SW12 1JB

— Your address, not name

91 Heron Avenue
Swanage
Dorset
BH12 4QA

8th May 2000 — Date

If you don't know the person's name

Dear Sir / Madam

I am writing to apply for the position of Air Steward which was advertised in the *Standard* on the 5th May.

At present I am working as a telephone sales operator for an international travel agency, where I have been working for the last two and a half years. As you can see from my CV, I have several years' experience of working in customer services with people of all ages and nationalities. I have a Travel and Tourism Diploma, and I can speak Spanish and French fluently. I visit Spain and France regularly, and I am a keen traveller.

— No contractions

I am motivated, enthusiastic, and keen to learn. I am good at working in a team. In addition, I am a qualified first-aider, and I am familiar with both Word and Lotus.

I enclose my CV. Please contact me at the above address if you require any further details. I look forward to hearing from you.

Dear Sir / Madam = Yours faithfully

Dear Mr White / Ms Black = Yours sincerely

Yours faithfully

Sign your name —

Jerry Warner

Jeremy Warner

2 Write a similar letter for one of the jobs on *p.70*.

Useful language

I am writing to apply for the position of …
At present I am working as …
As you can see from my CV …
I have (two years') experience of …
I am good at + *-ing* …
I enclose my CV / an application form.
Please contact me at the above address if …
I look forward to hearing from you.

29

Multi-word verbs

1 Complete the text.

> in a small village   ourselves   retiring
> in different countries   travelling   golf

> My parents are diplomats, and they've worked all over the world. It was strange for me and my sister growing up ¹ _____ , but it made us very independent − we can look after ² _____ . My father's looking forward to ³ _____ now. I think he's had enough of living abroad, and he wants to settle down ⁴ _____ and take up ⁵ _____ ! It'll be harder for my mum, I don't think she'll ever give up ⁶ _____ .

2 Write sentences about yourself with the multi-word verbs in the text.

The future

3 Match the questions and the answers.

1 What are you planning to do at the weekend?
2 What would you like to have for dinner?
3 Are you looking forward to Christmas?
4 Where are you going to go on holiday?
5 Why do you want to go to Madagascar?
6 How many books are you hoping to read on holiday?

a As many as I can!
b I don't really know, I just like the idea.
c Whatever's in the fridge.
d Not much. Too much food and family.
e Nothing much. Sleep!
f No idea. Somewhere warm and sunny.

Life plans

4 Complete the word web with these words.

> university   golf   children   leave home
> parties   cruise   retire   buy a house   gardening
> travel round the world   a better job

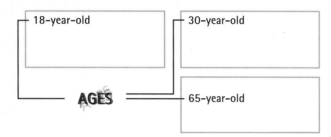

18-year-old

30-year-old

AGES

65-year-old

5 Make three sentences about each person in exercise 4.
Use *want to*, *'d like to*, *planning to*, *looking forward to*, and *going to*.
18-year-old   *I'm planning to travel round the world.*

6 Complete the texts.

Have you got a life plan?

Yes, definitely. I'm ¹g oing to finish university ²n_____ year, and after that I'm ³p_____ to get a job in banking or finance for a while, and earn lots of ⁴m_____ . Then I ⁵h_____ to set up my own business. I'd really ⁶l_____ to live in Scotland. I ⁷w_____ to get married and ⁸h_____ children, but that's not planned⁹y_____ !

Not really, no. The thing I'm ¹⁰l_____ _____ to most is finishing university and having some free ¹¹t_____ . I'd like to ¹²t_____ for a while – my girlfriend and I are ¹³p_____ a big trip to the Far East next ¹⁴y_____ . I ¹⁵d_____ _____ a job straight away – I'm ¹⁶g_____ to enjoy ¹⁷m_____ first.

30

Medical problems

1 Match the sentences with the problems.

> toothache   mosquito bites   sunburn
> short-sightedness   a cut finger   backache
> food poisoning   a cold

1 I think I did it playing tennis.
2 I've got a sore throat and a splitting headache.
3 I think it was the fish.
4 Open wide. I'm just going to give you an injection.
5 I knew I should have used suncream.
6 How many fingers am I holding up?
7 There were lots of them in my room last night.
8 I was just slicing a tomato.

At the chemist

2 Put the lines in order to make two conversations,
1–6 and a–f.

1	Can I help you?
☐	Thanks. I'll keep an eye on him.
☐	I won't, don't worry.
☐	You could try camomile lotion, or some aloe vera gel – that's very soothing.
☐	Fine. If he starts to feel sick, take him to the doctor.
☐	The lemon drink sounds good – I'll take the large size.
☐	Can I help you?
☐	Yes, I think I've got flu.
☐	I'll take the gel, please.
☐	Oh, dear. Well, you could try aspirin, or maybe this hot lemon drink with paracetamol.
2	Yes, I need something for my son. He's got very bad sunburn.
☐	And you should stay in bed – definitely don't go to work.

3 Write another dialogue with these words.
wife / sore throat
aspirin / throat pastilles
worse / doctor

31

Parts of the body

1 Match the numbers and the parts of the body.

☐ head	☐ body	☐ arm	☐ leg
☐ hand	☐ finger	☐ thumb	☐ ankle
☐ knee	☐ elbow	☐ foot	☐ shoulder

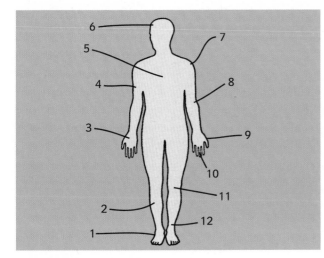

2 Complete these expressions.

my leg	an eye	fingers	headed	foot

1 _____ crossed!
2 I put my _____ in it.
3 He's really big-_____ .
4 You're pulling _____ .
5 Can you keep _____ on my bag?

3 Match the expressions in exercise 2 with these responses.

a No, I'm serious.
b Sure. Don't be long.
c Why, what did you say?
d Yes, we need all the luck we can get!
e I know – it's annoying, isn't it?

-ed and *-ing* adjectives

4 Choose the correct word.

1 The salary increase is very **disappointed** / (**disappointing**.)
2 I'm **bored** / **boring** with this film. It's awful. Shall we leave?
3 They are getting married tomorrow and she's so **excited** / **exciting**.
4 Your exam results are very good. You must be **pleased** / **pleasing**.
5 Don't you think English grammar is **confusing** / **confused**?
6 I always feel very **embarrassed** / **embarrassing** when I make a mistake in English.
7 It was a **terrified** / **terrifying** experience – I nearly died!
8 They're getting divorced. I'm **astonished** / **astonishing** – I thought they were the perfect couple.

32

Useful expressions

1 Read tapescript 32.2 on *p.111*. Complete these sentences.

1 _____ work to do?
2 Too busy to take the weekend _____ ?
3 _____ lots of people feel stressed.
4 There are many symptoms of stress, _____ headaches, tiredness, or backache.

Stress vocabulary

2 Are these adjectives positive, negative, or neutral?

nervous relaxed worried calm bored irritated
busy angry impatient frightened excited
energetic patient stressed

+	–	?
		nervous

Stress questionnaire

If you're competitive and easily bored, you'll probably suffer more from stress than if you're relaxed and patient. Do this quiz to see what personality type you are.

1 = never 2 = sometimes 3 = usually 4 = always

1	☐	I get angry whenever I have to queue for more than 15 minutes.
2	☐	I find it difficult to relax.
3	☐	I become annoyed when people speak too slowly.
4	☐	I'm happy to work under pressure.
5	☐	I get bored whenever I'm sitting quietly.
6	☐	I feel excited and energetic when I've been under pressure.
7	☐	I do things quickly when there is no rush.
8	☐	I interrupt people when I think they're wrong.
9	☐	I keep very busy at weekends.
10	☐	I interrupt other people's conversation in order to speed things up.

Now add up your score. Do you agree with your description?

10–20	You take life as it comes and don't let things worry you.
20–30	You have a mixed character. You know how to relax, but take some things seriously and can be competitive.
30–40	Your stress level is unhealthy, and you need to change your behaviour.

TAPESCRIPTS

02 SOCIAL LIFE

Oliver Are you doing anything this evening?
Holly No, nothing special.
Oliver Well, we're going to that new Chinese restaurant near the station. Would you like to come?
Holly Yes, that would be nice. What time are you going?
Oliver About 8.00. Shall we come and pick you up?
Holly Yes, great.
Oliver OK, I'll call for you at 7.30.

1 A What shall we do this weekend?
   B How about going to London on Saturday? There's a good exhibition on at the Royal Academy.
   A OK, that's a good idea. Shall we get the coach or the train?
   B Let's get the coach – it's cheaper.
   A Fine. What time?
   B Not too early. About 1.00 ish?
   A Yes, that would be great.
2 A Hello?
   B Hi, it's Charlie here.
   A Oh hi, Charlie, how's it going?
   B Oh, not bad. Look, do you fancy seeing a film this evening?
   A Good idea – I'd love to.
   B OK. Well, why don't we meet in the White Horse at 7.00, and then we can decide what we want to see?
   A OK, see you there. 7.00.
   B Right, bye.
   A Bye.

1 A How about going to the theatre tonight?
   B I'm afraid I can't – I'm going out for dinner.
2 A Let's go for a long walk this afternoon!
   B I'd love to, but I have to study for my exams.
3 A Why don't we go to the pub this evening?
   B I'm afraid I'm a bit busy – I'm staying at work till 10.00.
4 A Do you fancy going to a concert of Irish music?
   B I don't really like folk. How about the cinema instead?

04 NEAREST & DEAREST

Let me see ... I share my office with Jack and Phil and ... oh, and Colin Sanders works in the office next door.

Norman and Maureen – I haven't known them long. They moved in next door three months ago, but Mrs Anderson, bless her, has been at number 21 for years and years.

Now, well, John and I have been married for twelve years – hard to believe! Louise is nearly eleven now, our Sam's eight, and so is Muffin, our Siamese cat.

Stella ... she's my oldest friend. We went to school together. Mark and Julia are John's best friends, we see them most weekends, I suppose.

1 She's my best friend. She comes into my bedroom every morning and jumps onto my bed. She's always happy to see me, which is nice. She loves hiding under a newspaper and rushing in and out, round and round. She's done that since she was a kitten. And if I'm upset, and I go to my room, she follows me. I tell her all my problems and she listens, you know.
2 They're a nice couple. We're at 18 and they're at 20, next door. They keep themselves to themselves – sometimes I meet them when I'm going out to work in the morning, and we say hello, but otherwise I don't see much of them. They keep their house and garden really neat and tidy. We get on fine.
3 We sometimes argue, because we share an office, and I think if you share an office you get on each other's nerves a bit. You know, stupid things, like should the window be open or closed, should the heating be on or off, whose turn it is to wash the cups, that sort of thing ... Most of the time we get on OK.
4 I want him to be tall, dark, and handsome! He has to be young-ish, in his 20s, with big brown eyes. He has to dress well – you know, nice clothes, not necessarily expensive. And he should be kind and considerate, and listen to what I have to say, and respect my opinions.
5 We knew each other for years before we started going out together. It wasn't exactly love at first sight! But we get on really well, we never argue, our friends can't believe it! I was a bit worried when we decided to get married last year – I thought it would change things, but it's been fine.

06 ON THE ROAD

1 Flight BA 712 for Miami, Florida, is now boarding at gate 93. Flight BA 712 for Miami, Florida, is now boarding at gate 93.
2 Good afternoon, ladies and gentlemen. This is the 10.46 Intercity 125 to Edinburgh, calling at York, Durham, Berwick, and Edinburgh Waverley station. Would any people not wishing to travel please leave the train now.
3 Mind the gap.
4 This is a security announcement. Would the owner of a black briefcase left in the Duty Free store please return and claim – the owner of a black briefcase please return to the Duty Free store and reclaim it – thank you.
5 This is your captain speaking again, folks. We're running into a little turbulence ahead. Could all passengers return to their seats and fasten their seatbelts. Thank you.

6 Would all drivers please proceed to the car decks and return to their vehicles, as we will be docking shortly. Would all drivers please proceed to the car decks and return to their vehicles, as we will be docking shortly. Foot passengers may proceed to deck 2.
7 That'll be five fifty, please.
8 Tickets, please.
9 The next station is Piccadilly Circus. Change at Piccadilly Circus for the Bakerloo line.
10 Hastings, this is Hastings. This service terminates here. All change, please. Passengers wishing to travel to Ashford please proceed to platform 1. Hastings, this is Hastings. This service terminates here.

A Hello, National Rail Enquiries, Tracy speaking, how may I help you?
B Oh hello, I'd like to ask about trains from London to Edinburgh.
A When for?
B This Sunday, at around 10.00.
A Hold on a second ... right, there's one at 10.00 from King's Cross, which reaches Edinburgh at 3.21, or there's one at 10.30 which gets in at 4.06.
B And how much is it?
A Single or return?
B Return, please.
A First or standard?
B Oh, standard.
A That's £66.00, and there are no time restrictions on that ticket.
B OK, thanks very much.
A Thanks for calling. Bye.

Receptionist Good evening madam, how can I help you?
Guest Hello, can you tell me if you have any free rooms?
Receptionist One moment, I'll just check.
Guest Thank you.
Receptionist How many nights would you like to stay?
Guest Two.
Receptionist Would you like a single, a double, or a twin?
Guest A double please, en suite if possible.
Receptionist Yes, we have a double en suite deluxe.
Guest How much is that for two nights?
Receptionist For two nights that's £250.
Guest Does that include breakfast?
Receptionist Yes, a continental breakfast.
Guest OK, well that's fine.
Receptionist Very good. Could you fill in this card, please?

07 ENJOY YOUR TRIP!

1 A You look tired.
  B Yes, we got back at 3.00 this morning.
2 A There are lots of mosquitoes.
  B Well, put on some insect repellent.
3 A Are you taking a torch or candles?
  B I can't make up my mind.
4 A Are you leaving tomorrow?
  B Yes, I'm really looking forward to it.
5 A Are the photos ready?
  B Yes, I'm going to pick them up this afternoon.
6 A It's 9.00.
  B 9.00? We should set off for the airport.
7 A I'm cold.
  B You should get into your sleeping bag.

08 TRAVELLERS' TALES

Thank you for calling the Foreign and Commonwealth Office travel advice unit. We give advice on travel safety overseas. We have recorded information on the following countries: Egypt, the Gambia, India, Jamaica, Kenya, Nigeria, Pakistan, South Africa, Sri Lanka, and the USA. To hear the list again please press 1. For Egypt to Kenya please press 2. For Nigeria to the USA please press 3. For the USA press 7 now.

It is very important that travellers to the United States take out travel insurance.

Florida

If staying in a hotel, do not leave your door open at any time.

Do not wear expensive jewellery and avoid walking in run-down areas.

If arriving at night, take a taxi to your hotel and collect your hire car the next day.

If departing on an evening flight do not leave luggage and souvenirs in view in your hire car during the day. Thieves are looking for these vehicles and stealing the contents.

Drive on main highways and use well-lit car parks.

Do not stop if your car is bumped from behind. Instead, indicate to the other driver to follow you to the nearest public area and call for police assistance.

Do not sleep in your car on the roadside or in rest areas.

Emma Chris! How was the holiday?
Chris Don't ask.
Emma Why? What happened? Wasn't it 'the holiday of a lifetime'?
Chris It was absolutely fantastic. We went everywhere – Disneyworld, the Epcot centre, the Kennedy Space Centre. The kids had a great time, Amanda had a great time, and for once so did I ... until the last day, anyway.
Emma Why, what happened?
Chris We got robbed! Would you believe we were robbed by highway robbers. Highway robbers in the 21st century! And they were very polite – it was like a game to them.
Emma Highway robbers?
Chris Yes, it was really bad luck. We'd been really careful during the holiday, and we never really felt at all uncomfortable. Everywhere we went people were very polite, and friendly, and helpful. We just relaxed and enjoyed the holiday.
Emma And?

Chris Well, it all happened on the way home. We were driving to the airport – I'd finally got used to driving on the wrong side of the road – when suddenly a big old car bumped into the back of us. It happened so fast – the kids were thrown back into their seats and Amanda screamed. I didn't really know what was happening. Anyway, before I had time to do anything, he bumped me again. I was pretty angry, I can tell you. I stopped the car and so did he. I wasn't really thinking, I just got out of the car and started calling him an idiot. That's when I saw four big guys getting out, and one of them had a baseball bat.
Emma Ouch!
Chris Exactly. I thought 'it looks like I'll be needing the medical insurance after all', but no. The guy with the bat just said 'Now stay cool and you won't get hurt. We'll just empty the trunk and be on our way.' It took me a second to realize he meant the 'boot' and that he was going to rob us.
Emma You're joking.
Chris I wish I was. Anyway, they told Amanda and the kids to stay in the car, not that they were going to get out, and told me to open the boot. They took everything out of it – the luggage, of course, our coats, even the spare tyre. They didn't take our souvenirs and things – they were in the back with the kids. And then they put everything into their car and drove off.
Emma So Amanda and the kids were OK?
Chris Oh yes. We were all fine – a bit shaken up but fine. It didn't take long for the police to arrive. They looked after us, got us to the airport on time and so on, but it was a terrible way to end the holiday.

10 IT'S FOR YOU

1 The person you are calling knows you are waiting. Please hold the line while we try to connect you.
2 *a phone ringing*
3 The Vodaphone you have called may be switched off. Please try later.
4 Hello. This is Mike's phone speaking. If you leave a message, I'll get back to you. Please speak after you hear a series of beeps followed by a long tone. Thank you.
5 The number called has been changed to telephone number 01865 242450.
6 Elizabeth is not in her office right now. If you want to leave a message, press one. If you want to speak to someone else, please hold the line.
7 *engaged tone*
8 Thank you for calling the National Institute for Medical Research. You are held in a queue for the operator. If you know the extension you wish to reach, please dial it now.
9 Thank you for calling British Rail. Your call is in a queue and will be answered shortly ... we are sorry to keep you waiting, all our operators are busy, please hold the line.
10 The number you have dialled has not been recognized. Please check and try again.

A International Shipping, Elaine speaking, how may I help you?
B Could I speak to Bob Harris, please?
A Could I ask who's calling?
B Allan MacFarlane.
A Hold on a moment please, Mr MacFarlane.
B Thank you.

A I'm sorry, he's engaged at the moment. Will you hold?
B No, thanks, I'll ring back later.
A Would you like to leave a message?
B Could you tell him Allan called?
A Certainly Mr MacFarlane, I'll tell him.
B Thanks very much. Goodbye.

A International Shipping, Elaine speaking, how may I help you?
B Could I speak to Bob Harris, please?
A Could I ask who's calling?
B Allan MacFarlane.
A Hold on a moment please, Mr MacFarlane. I'll just put you through.
B Thank you.
C Bob Harris speaking.
B Hello Bob, it's Allan, I'm just ringing to confirm that I'll be arriving in the afternoon ...

A Hello?
B Hello. Can I speak to Chris, please?
A Who is it?
B It's Mark.
A Hello, Mark. Hang on a second, I'll just get her. I think she's gone out. She'll be back soon.
B OK, not to worry. I'll phone back later.
A Can I give her a message?
B Just tell her I called.
A OK. Bye.
B Bye.

11 TALK TO ME

1 amanda@rad.net.id
2 106762.1927@compuserve.com
3 info@earthwatch.org
4 www.timenet.co.uk
5 www.usatoday.com
6 www.guardian.co.uk

12 OUT OF TOUCH

Amanda OK, number one, 'Let *me* look at the map'. What's that, Russell?
Russell I think they're in a car. I think it's a man ...
Amanda Yeah, I agree. They're in the car, a woman's driving. Number two. 'How do I look?' Woman to man?
Russell Definitely. Just about to go out for the evening.
Amanda That's what I think ... woman to man, asking him how ... how she looks, cos a man doesn't care how he looks. Number three, 'Come on! Hurry up!'
Russell Oh, that's me! Er ... that's definitely a man because er ... as you know, Amanda, women are always late!
Amanda I don't agree with that! That's rubbish! Right, number four 'But you never do the washing up' ... definitely a woman saying that, cos men never wash up.
Russell I don't ... I disagree with that completely.
Amanda That's what I think! 'Where did I put the car keys?' Man. Definitely a man, cos they always lose them.
Russell It's always the man who asks that, I agree with that.
Amanda Yeah.
Russell 'We never go out any more.'
Amanda No, no, you missed one. 'Do you want to talk about it?' Do you want to talk about it?!

Russell	That's a woman. It's a woman asking, 'Do you want to talk about it?'
Amanda	Yeah, that's what I think ... definitely a woman. Anyway, men never want to talk about it! 'We never go out any more'. Woman. Complaining to her, her boyfriend, yeah.
Russell	That's usually ... when the, erm, the World Cup is on the television, don't you think?
Amanda	Yeah, that's true! 'I love you, too'.
Russell	I think a man says that more than a woman, cos the woman is usually the one who says it first.
Amanda	Rubbish! That's not true. 'You're wearing a new shirt!' Woman to man. Cos men don't notice new shirts.
Russell	Correct! I agree with that.
Amanda	'I'll do it later'. I think that's a man.
Russell	So do I ... yeah, that's the man in response to a woman who's asked him to do the washing up.
Amanda	Yeah, yeah, he's saying 'I'll do it later', yeah that's it.

Interviewer	You may or may not agree that men and women are different in various ways – how they drive, what they eat and drink, the things they like doing. But one area which is less obvious is how they talk, and what they talk about ... Julian Manson, welcome. First, who talks more, women or men?
Julian	Well, according to the stereotype, women talk more than men. They like to chat, they like small talk, they like to gossip, and typically, married women always complain that their husbands don't talk to them enough. He sits and reads the newspaper or watches television. But studies have shown that men talk more than women, so in fact the stereotype is not true.
Interviewer	How can you explain that?
Julian	Men talk more in public ... at meetings, in discussions, in classrooms. Studies have shown that men speak more often in these situations, and for a longer time. Men's turns range from 10 to 17 seconds, while women's turns range from 3 to 10 seconds. So this in true in public situations. In private situations, it may be different.
Interviewer	What about differences in the ways that men and women talk?
Julian	I think that everyone knows that men and women have different ways of talking. The difficult thing is to say how they're different. Many people have studied men's and women's speech, and there do seem to be some linguistic differences.
Interviewer	Can you give us some examples?
Julian	Yes, well, a strange example is that women describe colours better than men – they use a wider vocabulary of colours. And there are grammatical differences as well as vocabulary.
Interviewer	Really?
Julian	Yes, women use more question tags like *it is, isn't it, you do, don't you, you would, wouldn't you?* Obviously everybody uses question tags all the time, but women do use slightly more. Men tend to use more imperatives – *do this, don't do that*. Women are more polite and tend to use phrases like

	Could you ... and *Do you mind?* Women also use more intensifiers with adjectives and adverbs, like *very, really, so. It's really lovely, it's so beautiful, I like him very much.* Some researchers say women apologize more.
Interviewer	Interesting! What about topics of conversation? Are there any differences there?
Julian	Men tend to exchange information in conversation, in a very factual kind of way. Women are more intimate – they share secrets. They talk about emotions and relationships far more, personal things, feelings, problems they have. Men tend to talk more about money, jobs, sport, less personal topics.
Interviewer	Really? I've never noticed that – my men friends talk to me about quite personal things.
Julian	That may be because you're a woman. Men with men don't usually talk about very personal things, but men with women are more personal, and women with women talk about the most personal areas. Also, it depends a lot on the individual, some men are happy talking about relationships, and some women aren't, so it's impossible to say exactly that 'Men are like this, and women are like that'.

14 READY TO ORDER

1 No, that's all, thanks.
2 That would be very helpful.
3 3.95, please.
4 Certainly, madam.
5 Well done, please.
6 Here you are.
7 No, thanks, we'll have mineral water.
8 No, thanks, I really couldn't.

Waiter	Are you ready to order, sir?
Man	Yes, I think so. Darling?
Woman	I'll have the vegetable soup to start ...
Waiter	The vegetable soup. And to follow, madam?
Woman	The salmon with a salad.
Waiter	And for you, sir?
Man	I'll have the vegetable soup too, please.
Waiter	Two vegetable soups.
Man	And I'll have a steak, I think.
Waiter	How would you like it, sir? Rare, medium, or well done?
Man	Very rare – blue if you can.
Waiter	Thank you very much, sir. Would you like to see the wine list?

Waiter	Ready to order?
Customer	Yes, I'd like the potato soup.
Waiter	White or brown bread?
Customer	White, please.
Waiter	And to follow?
Customer	Just a chicken salad, please.
Waiter	And to drink?
Customer	A mineral water.
Waiter	Still or sparkling?
Customer	Sparkling, please.
Waiter	Ice and lemon?
Customer	Both, please.

16 SHOP TILL YOU DROP

Roger	One of the things I really loved about Spain was the bars. They were open early in the morning, for a coffee on your way to work, until the early hours of the next morning. It was great!
Teresa	In the Czech Republic the opening hours are better than in Britain, I mean small shops open early, at 7 or 8, and close late, at 6 or 7.
Anna	Why does everything close so early in Britain? I mean I can't believe they asked us to leave the restaurant because they were closing. 11.00 and it's 'I'm sorry, we're closing'. 'Last orders, please'. I mean after 11 there's nowhere to go, it's terrible.

Shopping; Changing Times

Good afternoon, shoppers. It's 5.25. The store will be closing in five minutes. Five minutes, thank you.

Not long ago shops in Britain opened at 9.00 and closed at 5.30. That was how it was. If people wanted to go shopping they had to go at lunchtime, or in the thirty minutes between finishing work and the shops closing. Shops opening when people needed them? Never! Nothing was open on Sundays – Sunday was a day for cleaning the car, doing the garden, and spending time with the family. But now shopping in Britain is changing, and changing fast. Why? Partly because of the main supermarket chains, which started to open some of their stores from 8.00 in the morning until 10.00 in the evening.

Woman 1	I prefer to go in the evening, it's quieter and more relaxed and there isn't so much traffic on the roads. I don't know, it's just much less stressful – I don't like driving during the day. Although of course, now everyone does their shopping in the evening, so it's getting busy again.
Man 1	I haven't got time during the day, so I always come after work, about 7.00 or 8.00. I hate doing the shopping whatever time it is, I can't stand all the people ...

The number of people doing their shopping in the evenings has increased dramatically. And the supermarkets now open their doors on Sundays, too. Lots of people said it was terrible, that Sundays should be a day of rest, and that nobody would want to go to the shops – but they were wrong.

Woman 2	I work six days a week, so I can only come on Sundays. Yeah, I think it's great. I sometimes bring the family, and we shop together, it's like a day out. The kids really like it.

And now, some supermarkets are open 24 hours a day. But who would do their shopping while the rest of us are sleeping? Who would we find filling their trolleys in the small hours?

Young women	Yes, I suppose 2.30 is a strange time to go shopping. We've been to a club and we're going home. The supermarket is right next to the main road, so we thought we'd come in and get something for breakfast, you know ... usually we don't mind when we shop, we're students so we can come anytime ...
Man 2	Well, I haven't been sleeping very well, and I woke up *again* and I felt a bit hungry, and there was nothing in the fridge so I thought well, why not, I'll do the shopping. There's nobody here, is there? I quite like it. I wouldn't normally be here at 3.00 in the morning.

Shopping in Britain is certainly changing. Sundays aren't special any more, they're just like any other day of the week. Go to any city centre on a Sunday and you'll find shops open and shoppers spending money. But at least the British still want to go to the shops – in a few years' time, all the shops might be empty, and everyone will be at home, sitting in front of the computer, credit cards by their side ...

18 WHEN IN ROME

1 A Would you like a cup of coffee?
  B Thanks, that'd be lovely.
2 A Hello, how are you?
  B I'm fine, thanks. And you?
3 A Could I have some aspirin, please?
  B Would you like 24 or 48?
4 A Excuse me, do you know the way to the stadium?
  B I'm afraid I don't. I'm a stranger here myself. Sorry.
5 A Have you got the time, please?
  B It's ten past ten.
6 A My phone number's 0161 7663339.
  B Sorry, you couldn't repeat that, could you?
7 A Richard, can I introduce you to Nicola Rendall?
  B Pleased to meet you, Nicola.
8 A It's a lovely day, isn't it?
  B Yes, beautiful.

19 LET'S CELEBRATE

1 I'm 26 today.
2 We're going to have a baby!
3 *clock striking, followed by cheering*
4 I've got my driving test tomorrow.
5 *carol singers*
6 Cheers.
7 We've been married for 25 years today.

20 LIVING ABROAD

1

Interviewer What's the best thing about living in Britain?
Thérèse The best thing? I would say ... my relationship with my boyfriend.
Interviewer What's the worst thing?
Thérèse Being in Britain! No, I don't know, I think the worst thing is the food ... and the coffee, oh yes, the coffee.
Interviewer What do you miss most about France?
Thérèse Well, first of all my family, second my food, and third my friends ... my friends most of all.
Interviewer What's the strangest thing about living in Britain?
Thérèse The strangest thing ... I found it very strange, I still find it very strange that the pubs close at 11 o'clock ... and the fact that you can't go into a bar just to ... you can't really go into a bar just to have a cup of tea or coffee or you know, at 7 o'clock at night, I find it a little bit strange.
Interviewer What advice would you give someone coming to live in Britain?
Thérèse A French person? If ... What would it be? Bring an umbrella.

3

Interviewer What was the best thing about living in Ecuador?
Jim The best thing for me I think was the mountains, I loved the mountains.
Interviewer And what was the worst thing?
Jim I don't think there was a worst thing really, I just liked everything about it.
Interviewer What did you miss most about England?
Jim What did I miss most? My bed and er ... probably family and friends because I couldn't afford to come home for Christmas.
Interviewer What was the strangest thing about living in Ecuador?
Jim The strangest thing? Being rich! I mean even on my salary I could afford to do things, like, like ... fly somewhere for the weekend.
Interviewer What advice would you give someone going to live in Ecuador?
Jim Travel around as much as they can, it's an amazing place ...

4

Andrew Well, congratulations on your new job. Are you looking forward to it?
Jim Yes, a lot, but you know, it's always difficult moving to a new country.
Andrew Oh, I'm sure you'll be fine.
Jim Well, look, you've lived in Sri Lanka, haven't you, so I wanted to ask you some advice.
Andrew Sure, go ahead.
Jim What do I need to take?
Andrew Take with you, you mean? Well ... you can get most things out there, so you don't really need to take much. You can get really cheap clothes there, you know, cotton shirts and trousers. Shoes are more difficult, so I'd recommend that you take as many pairs as possible ... a couple of pairs of good work shoes, some casual shoes, and maybe a couple of pairs of trainers or sports shoes if you're going to play tennis or squash or that kind of thing. Umm ...
Jim So do you think I need to take a coat or jumper with me or anything like that?
Andrew No, no. It's really hot, really, really hot out there, but I guess you'll need a jacket or a jumper to wear if you go up into the hills or anything, then it can get a bit cool, particularly in the evenings, but in the city it's pretty hot all year round.
Jim How much did you pack when you went there?
Andrew Not much, hardly anything. I took one really small suitcase with me, with just a few clothes. When I came back, I had loads of stuff ... but when I went, I tried to take as little as possible. I did take quite a lot of books, but in fact it's very easy to get English books there, so you don't need to take any.
Jim Anything else you can think of?
Andrew Yes, take a couple of spare pairs of glasses, just in case yours get lost or stolen.
Jim Is it safe? What's it like in terms of stuff getting stolen, things like that?
Andrew Oh it's quite a safe place ... be careful with your money, and your camera, and things like that, your personal possessions, just like anywhere. But people are very friendly, and it's a very busy place, so even at night there are people around, walking about, selling food.

Jim What's the food like?
Andrew Very hot, and there's lots of rice! There's lots of fresh fruit, fantastic fruit, all kinds of different bananas, long ones, short ones, mangoes, papaya, coconut ... you'll be OK if you're careful, most places are very clean, you won't have any problems.
Jim What about the water, is it safe to drink?
Andrew No, I always used bottled water, even to clean my teeth.

22 JUST LOOKING

1 Excuse me, can you tell me where the CDs are, please?
2 Excuse me, do you think I could try this on?
3 I'd like to buy a new battery for my watch.
4 Two for *Casablanca*, please.
5 Excuse me, could you tell me where I can find the toothpaste, please?
6 Can I have a phonecard, please?
7 Could you tell me what kind of film I need?
8 Could you possibly dry clean these trousers in one hour?
9 Can I help you?
10 Could I make an appointment for this afternoon, please?

Assistant Hello, can I help you?
Customer Yes, have you got this in a size 12?
Assistant In blue?
Customer Yes, in blue.
Assistant I'll just have a look. Yes, here you are.
Customer Could I try it on, please?
Assistant Of course. The fitting rooms are over there.
Customer Thank you.

Assistant Any good?
Customer I think it's a bit tight. Do you think I could try on a bigger one?
Assistant Yes, I'll see if we've got a 14.

Assistant Better?
Customer Yes, I'll take it.
Assistant Great, OK, if you could take it to the cash desk.

Cashier How would you like to pay?
Customer Cash, please.
Cashier That'll be 15.99, then.
Customer There you are.
Cashier 16, 17, 18, 19, 20. Thanks. Your receipt's in the bag. Goodbye.
Customer Thanks very much. Bye.

1 Could I try it on, please?
2 Can you tell me where the shampoo is?
3 I'd like to buy a phonecard, please.
4 Can I pay by credit card?
5 Could you possibly dry clean this suit today?
6 Could you tell me how much this is?
7 Can I try a smaller one, please?
8 Could you tell me where the fitting rooms are?

24 MY GENERATION

The Chernobyl nuclear accident happened in 1986.
John Lennon was killed in 1980.
Björn Borg won Wimbledon from 1976-80.
Mother Teresa died in 1997.
Neil Armstrong walked on the moon in 1969.
Martin Luther King was assassinated in1968.
The Berlin Wall was demolished in 1989.

Keith The Berlin Wall was knocked down ... now I remember this because my girlfriend, erm, my girlfriend went to Berlin and brought back a piece of the Berlin Wall.

Sara A piece of the wall! So what year was that, eighty ...

Keith I think it was nineteen ... ninety.

Sara Nineteen ninety?

Keith I think so.

Sara Mmm OK. Now, John Lennon was killed ... um, was it the late seventies? No, no, early eighties.

Keith No.

Sara Eighty ... one. Eighty-two.

Keith I'm trying to remember what happened, where I was and what happened.

Sara I don't know, early eighties, I can't remember, I think I was still at school.

Keith Maybe it was eighty-seven, eighty-eight.

Sara That late?

Keith I think so. I may be wrong, may be wrong.

Sara Mother Teresa died, that was nineteen ninety-seven. It was August or September, just a couple of days after Diana died, and there'd been a huge fuss ...

Keith That's right, that's right. And the years that Borg won Wimbledon was definitely the late seventies ... no, no, mid-seventies, wasn't it?

Sara Something like that ... no, late seventies, I think. The last time he won it was in eighty-one so ... and he won it five times in a row, didn't he?

Keith Let's say seventy-seven to eighty-one?

Sara Yeah. Nineteen sixty-seven, Neil Armstrong?

Keith On the moon ... yeah, I think it was nineteen sixty-seven.

Sara And Martin Luther King sixty ... eight. I'd say sixty, sixty-eight.

Keith It's around there, late sixties.

Sara Chernobyl.

Keith Chernobyl, oh that was nineteen eighty-six or seven, wasn't it?

Sara No idea. Mid-eighties.

Keith Mid-eighties.

1

Susan Look at this photo. I can't believe we looked like that!

Dave I know, it's so embarrassing, isn't it? Look at my hair!

Susan Yeah, well, the thing was everybody used to look like that. I think people followed fashion more in those days, now they look more different. Then, if long hair was in fashion, everybody had long hair ...

Dave Including the men! I really can't believe it. I'd forgotten how long it used to be. And my shirt. That is a *horrible* shirt.

Susan Well, I'm no better! Look at that dress, and all the flowers! I can't imagine wearing clothes like that. When do you think this was taken?

Dave Umm, I'd say about 19 ... 68, I was about 22 then, I'd just finished university, and I was wondering what to do with my life. I didn't think I'd end up in a bank!

Susan Yeah, the late sixties were exciting times, weren't they? I mean Neil Armstrong on the moon, Martin Luther King, the students in Paris, and England were good at football. It felt as if the world was really changing fast.

Dave Yeah, and the music and everything. The Beatles, the Rolling Stones, Bob Dylan. It was a good time to be young ...

2

Sam Well, we haven't changed that much.

Daniel Not really, no. I've still got that hat ...

Sam But not those stupid sunglasses! Oh, my hair was a lot shorter then. And I don't wear a nose ring any more. I don't think I'd have got my job with a nose ring!

Daniel Well, it was really fashionable, wasn't it, to have nose rings, and we were both students then, so we could wear what we liked, really. It's a bit different now we've both got jobs.

Sam So when was this photo taken?

Daniel Oh, 97 I think, in the summer. Or was it 98? No, it wasn't 98 because there was the World Cup in France that year, and I wore my England T-shirt all summer!

Sam I remember that T-shirt.

Daniel I think this was just after Diana died ...

Sam I remember, that was really sad, wasn't it?

Daniel Yeah, all those flowers in London, and that Elton John song ...

25 BEING A WORKER

1 A Are Jack and Chloe around?

B Not at the moment, they're taking the dog for a walk.

2 A Have you seen David?

B I think he's outside, cleaning the car.

3 A Hello, could I speak to Stephanie, please?

B I'm afraid she's not in – she's doing the shopping. Do you want to leave a message?

4 A Hi, Mike. What are you up to?

B Oh, I'm studying for my exams next week.

5 A What are John and Sara doing?

B They're playing tennis.

6 A Do you know where Kate is?

B She's having a shower, I think. She won't be long.

26 ALL WORK AND NO PLAY

1 I'm afraid of flying and my boss has asked me to fly to Paris for a meeting.

2 I'm so worried about my exams that I can't sleep.

3 I borrowed a colleague's car yesterday and I had an accident.

4 There's a party tonight but I've got loads of work to do.

5 I'm thinking about leaving my job – it pays well but it's really boring.

Jane I've got a real problem – I'm afraid of flying and my boss has asked me to fly to Paris for a meeting. What do you think I should do?

Owen When's the meeting?

Jane Monday morning at 10.00.

Owen Well, if I were you, I'd go by train on Sunday. Then you can see a bit of Paris, too.

Jane Good idea! Thanks.

28 JUST THE JOB

Number one – yes, this is good advice. But actually we have an interview room with a table and chairs, so I don't need to prepare it – it's always ready.

The second point. Yes, now this is important. I ask them if they'd like a cup of tea or coffee, and yes, I chat about their journey. How they got here, did it take a long time? That sort of thing, just to get them talking.

Number three – ah now, it says 'Don't make a decision in the first minute', but I *do* make quick

decisions. I always know in the first minute if I like someone. I know I shouldn't but I do.

Number four – difficult questions? Well, maybe it's a good idea to ask difficult questions, but in my experience people don't like them. Questions about money, about themselves, what sort of person they are, that sort of thing. It's funny how people don't like to talk about themselves, isn't it?

And number five – a quick decision? Well, we always, always tell people in writing. After the interview I fill in a form, and this is used to write a standard letter, offering the job – or not of course – so I suppose people usually know the following day.

1 Why do you want to work for us?
2 Who will I work with?
3 How much do you earn in your current job?
4 How much will I earn?
5 What are your strengths and weaknesses?
6 Why do you think you'd be good at this job?
7 What are the training opportunities?
8 Where do you want to be in five years' time?
9 Do you like working in a team?
10 Is it possible to work flexitime?

Interview 1

Applicant A bit of cinema, a bit of reading, you know ... I don't really have very much free time, really. In my current job I quite often have to work on Saturdays and Sundays, or late at night when the computers can be turned off – we sometimes can't do much during the day because everyone's using their machines.

Interviewer OK, great. Perhaps we can turn to this job now. First of all, why do you want to work for us?

Applicant I think because yours in the biggest company in the field. I'm really interested in modern communications, and the biggest company should offer the biggest opportunities.

Interviewer And what are your strengths and weaknesses?

Applicant Weaknesses? I haven't got any! And strengths? Ambition. I really want to do well, and I'm flexible and reliable.

Interviewer Why do you think you'd be good at this job?

Applicant Oh, um, why would I be good? I don't know really ... I just think I'd be good at it, I mean, I know a lot about systems support, and this seems to be the perfect job for me.

Interviewer Where do you want to be in five years' time?

Applicant I want to progress within the organization – I'd like more responsibility, and more money too, if possible!

Interviewer Speaking of money, could I ask you a few details about your current salary and extras?

Applicant Yes, sure. Well, I'm earning 19,000 at the moment, but then I get some overtime on top of that, so I suppose altogether it comes to more like twenty-two. And I'm a member of the company pension scheme which is good for the future ...

Interview 2

Applicant Yeah, the traffic was terrible, and the weather, it took me ages to get here, and then I couldn't find the car park! I'll just put my umbrella in the corner here, shall I? Anyway, I'm really sorry I'm late.

Interviewer Well, I'm glad you got here in the end. Now, we should probably get going as fast as we can, because I've got another interview at 12.00. I think the most important question I can ask is 'Why do you want to work for us?'

Applicant Well, I'm a bit bored where I'm working at the moment, so I'd really like a change. I mean, I've been there for nearly a year now. I don't know if I'll like it more here, but it's a bigger company, and the salary's a lot better than the job I've got. Also, I like the idea of flexitime, because I find it really hard to get up in the morning!

Interviewer And what would you say your main strengths and weaknesses are?

Applicant Strengths? A sense of humour. And weaknesses? Well, everybody says I'm really disorganized, but I don't think I am. I'm sometimes a bit late, you know, for meetings and deadlines, but I usually survive! I think I'm reliable – I always do what I say I'm going to do, eventually.

Interviewer Why do you think you'd be good at this job?

Applicant Oh ... hmm, that's a difficult question. Well, I've got the right qualifications, I'm interested, and I like a challenge. I'm quite independent, too.

Interviewer And where do you want to be in five years' time?

Applicant Australia, I hope! I mean I'm planning to stay in Britain for a year or two, but to be honest I really want to move somewhere hot and sunny. And after a couple of years I'll probably feel like another change.

Interviewer OK. And what about your free time? What sort of things do you do?

Applicant Um, well, I like to keep my weekends completely free – I hate having, having to work at the weekend, because I go walking. I try to get up to Scotland whenever I can. And I play a lot of sport, tennis, squash, things like that, you know ...

30 GET WELL SOON

Helen Hi, Nick. You don't look too good.
Nick No, I feel terrible.
Helen What's the matter?
Nick I've got a splitting headache and my body aches all over.
Helen Oh dear. It sounds like flu to me. Why don't you go home?
Nick Too much work to do ...

1 A You don't look very well, are you all right?
  B Not really. I've got awful backache.
  A You poor thing. Do you want an aspirin?
  B No, thanks. I've just taken some. I'll be fine.
2 A You don't look very well. What's up?
  B No, I'm fine. I'm feeling a bit sick, that's all.
  A Do you want me to stop for a bit?
  B No, don't worry. It'll go soon.

3 A That's over 20 minutes now!
  B I know, but I can't stop.
  A Drink a glass of water very slowly – it always works for me.
  B OK, I'll try it ....

32 UNDER PRESSURE

Sharon I think, erm, work more than anything, being late for work, not earning enough money, going to work on the underground, you know. What do I do when I feel stressed? Eat chocolate, have a really long hot relaxing bath, with my, with some really soothing music playing and, and candles, and a lovely cup of tea. I just stay there for hours.

Brad It really stresses me out when, when my mother asks me, like you know, when I'm going to get married. She always says it in front of my girlfriends. Unbelievable. What do I do when I feel stressed? Erm, usually, I, well, if I'm really stressed out the best thing is if I go and have a game of squash, or do some weights, you know physical exercise, takes out the aggression.

Ben Um, I think phoning information lines, recorded information lines because you always get some stupid message. What do I do? I don't do anything really.

Interviewer Too much work to do? Working long hours? Taking work home? Too busy to take the weekend off? No holidays? No social life? *Stressed out*? Of course you are! Well, today on the Health Programme we have a guest who may have some interesting advice. Dr Janet Squire, author of *How to Beat Stress*. Welcome, Dr Squire.

Dr Squire Hello.
Interviewer Obviously lots of people feel stressed, but what exactly causes stress?

Dr Squire Well, you need to realize that there are two kinds of stress – *good* stress and *bad* stress. Good stress comes from situations where you feel in control. These situations are a challenge. Bad stress comes from situations where you feel out of control, and that could be when the washing machine breaks down, or when you go shopping and the supermarket is very crowded.

Interviewer How do I know if I'm suffering from stress?
Dr Squire Well, there are many symptoms of stress, such as headaches, tiredness, or backache. If you get angry easily, then you're probably suffering from stress.

Interviewer And so what can we do once we've identified that we suffer from stress?

Dr Squire Stress is like smoking – if you really want to stop, you can. By changing the way you think and the way you behave, you can reduce the amount of stress that you feel. You don't need to see a doctor, you don't need tranquillisers, and you don't need sleeping pills!

Interviewer Now in your book, you identify some exercises that people can do if they're feeling stressed. Tell us about some of these.

Dr Squire Well, exercise is one of the best things you can do for stress. How much exercise do you take? Not running or going to the gym, but ordinary, everyday exercise. Probably not much. Most people drive to work, take the lift to their office, and sit there all day. Try running up the stairs, and take a ten-minute walk at lunchtime. Some people find that doing very physical sports helps them to relax – it makes them feel energized and happy. It's very important to take breaks during the day and do the things that you want – even if it's just having lunch with a friend. I think it's also important to have fun ... spend a minute making a list of all the things that you enjoy doing, like reading a book or going to the cinema, and make sure that you do these things regularly.

Interviewer You also suggest some more unusual things, don't you?

Dr Squire Well, perhaps they might seem unusual because they're so obvious. Slow down your eating, for example. Put your knife and fork down between bites, and count to 20 while you chew your food. It'll give you time to talk and relax. If you slow down your eating, you'll find that you slow down in other areas of life. You should avoid too much coffee and too much alcohol – and you should eat healthy foods like vegetables, salads, and fruit – but more importantly you should enjoy eating. And finally try to spend a day without your watch. Make an effort to forget about time.

Interviewer Dr Squire, that's all we've got time for. Thanks for joining us. Coming up after the break it's ...

OXFORD
UNIVERSITY PRESS

Great Clarendon Street, Oxford OX2 6DP

Oxford University Press is a department of the University of Oxford. It furthers the University's objective of excellence in research, scholarship, and education by publishing worldwide in

Oxford New York

Athens Auckland Bangkok Bogotá
Buenos Aires Cape Town Chennai
Dar es Salaam Delhi Florence Hong Kong
Istanbul Karachi Kolkata Kuala Lumpur Madrid
Melbourne Mexico City Mumbay Nairobi
Paris São Paulo Shanghai Singapore Taipei
Tokyo Toronto Warsaw

with associated companies in Berlin Ibadan

Oxford and Oxford English are registered trade marks of Oxford University Press in the UK and in certain other countries

© Oxford University Press 2000

Database right Oxford University Press (maker)

First published 2000
Third impression 2001

ISBN 0-19-434074-0

Printed in Italy by Poligrafico Dehoniano

Acknowledgements

The Publisher and Authors would like to thank the following for their kind permission to use articles, extracts, or adaptations from copyright material:

p.7 'Speak for yourself' activity based on an idea from *Classroom Dynamics* by Jill Hadfield © Oxford University Press 1992.
p.20 Covers of Lonely Planet Guides to Zimbabwe, Botswana & Namibia, and Iceland, Greenland & the Faroe Islands reproduced by permission of Lonely Planet Publications.
p.22 Transcript from the Foreign and Commonwealth Office Travel Advice Line reproduced by permission of the Foreign and Commonwealth Office.
p.27 Recorded message reproduced by permission of British Rail.
p.27 British Telecommunications recorded messages reproduced by permission of British Telecommunications plc.
p.27 Recorded message reproduced by permission of the National Institute for Medical Research.
p.64 'When the perfect mother turns out to be Dad' by Angela Neustatter, *The Telegraph Magazine* 21 February 1998 © Angela Neustatter 1998.
p.80 Extract from *The Hitchhiker's Guide to the Galaxy* by Douglas Adams, Pan Macmillan 1988, reproduced by permission of Macmillan.

Every effort has been made to trace and contact copyright holders prior to publication, but in some cases this has not been possible. We apologize for any apparent infringement of copyright, and if notified, the publisher will be pleased to rectify any errors or omissions at the earliest opportunity.

Illustrations by:

Matthew Booth/the Art Market pp.18, 37, 59 (clothing); Stefan Chabluk pp.14, 22, 53, 86, 95; Graham Cox pp.6, 11, 21, 29, 39, 43, 51, 59 (man in jumper), 69, 79, 83; Ian Jackson pp.12, 23, 27, 36 (young man and bank manager), 56, 67, 74, 87, 89, 90, 97, 98, 101, 104; Peter Jones pp.7, 30, 46; Julian Mosedale/Pennant pp.4, 15, 16, 26, 28, 31, 36 (money bath), 61, 66, 72, 76, 88, 93, 94, 99, 100; Pierre-Paul Pariseau pp.33, 34, 44, 57, 60

Commissioned photography by:

Mark Mason and Graham Alder pp.20, 23 (baseball bat), 24 (handmade card by kind permission of the Henry-Butler Partnership), 37 (fast food), 42 (shop opening sign), 54 (magazine and Post-it note), 55 (timetables), 77 (weights)

Location photography by:

Maggy Milner pp.63, 73

The Publisher and Authors would like to thank the following for their kind permission to reproduce photographs:

The Anthony Blake Photo Library pp.37 (expensive restaurant), 77 (G.Buntrock); Bubbles Photo Library p.52 (J.Powell/man); Comstock Photo Library pp.50 (champagne), 71; Corbis p.62 (S.I.N./John Lennon); Ben Elwes p.64; Jane Havis p.4 (house); the Image Bank pp.8 (H.Sims), 17 (G.Rossi/bus), 32 (Color Day), 35 (S. McAlister), 50 (P-E.Berglund/candle), 53, 68 (Regine M/Auntie Ad) (M.Romanelli/Uncle Vice), 75 (Yellow Dog Prods/woman in checked shirt), (J.P.Kelly/grandfather), 78 (Turner & Davies); Impact Photos pp.9 (C.Moyse/pub sign), 17 (C.Coates/rickshaw), 47 (A.Smith/two young men), (G.Barraud/young man); the Kobal Collection p.58; Andrew Lamb p.81; Bruce McGowen and Kate Richardson p.13; Christine Osborne Pictures pp.17

(Thai beach guesthouse), 49; Oxford Scientific Films p.80 (K.Wothe/ants), (J.Brown/sheep), (D.J.Cox/eagle), (Gerard Soury/dolphins); Popperfoto pp.16, 62 (SAG/Mother Teresa), (Vision/Martin Luther King), (Reuters/Chernobyl); Rex Features pp.17 (G.Francis/ferry), 47 (Sipa Press/farmers sitting), 62 (C.Knight/Björn Borg), 63 (hippy couple); Run for Africa/Emma Bourne p.14; Sainsbury's Archives p.42 (J.Sainsbury's c.1910); Samsonite p.54 (luggage, © Samsonite); Frank Spooner Pictures p.62 (Gamma/Berlin Wall); Swatch/Bridgehouse Public Relations p.48; Telegraph Colour Library pp.5 (Masterfile/Winnipeg), 17 (D.Richards/hotel), 22 (J.M.Martin/flag), 50 (rose), 54 (M.Goldman/couple), 62 (Space Frontiers/man on moon), 75 (S.Powell/woman), 82 (Aitch/yoga), 89 (Bavaria-Bildagentur); Tony Stone Images pp.4 (I.O'Leary/mother & daughter), 5 (W.Hodges/man), 9 (D.YoungWolff/couple), 10 (C.Kunin/girl), (I.Shaw/grandfather), (R.Buchler/teenager), 17 (D.Jones/yacht), 17 (high speed train), 19 (K.Lahnstein), 23 (C.Sleicher/car), 26 (PBJ Pictures/couple), 41 (C.Everard), 42 (R.A.Butcher/modern supermarket), 45 (L.& B.Schlowsky), 50 (T.Flach/presents), 52 (S.McComb/woman), 55 (P.Correz/man with hat), 55 (Amwell/man swimming), 75 (B.Torrez/couple), 80 (T.Latham/dog), 82 (S.Werner/woman in supermarket), 104 (R.Krisel/woman & man)

The Publisher and Authors would like to thank the following for their feedback on the course:
Catherine Bond (freelance)
Jane Hudson (Cambridge House, Madrid, Spain)

Vic and Bruce would like to thank Amanda for her critical eye and unfailing support, Silvana for her detailed review and comments, and all the staff, trainees, and students who were interviewed and recorded during the writing of this book (International House, Hastings, June 1998 to January 1999), especially Teresa, Thérèse, Susan, and Peter. They would also like to thank Kate and the Grundys for their contributions, Ben for fixing the computer, Thomson and Martinet … and Jason Lombard.